By the Grace of God
I AM WHAT I AM

To Freda,
May the Light of Jesus continue to
shine in and through you in everything you
do, in every place you go. (2 Cor. 2:14)

JEFF PATE

Jeff Pate
July 2007

DIAKONIA

BY THE GRACE OF GOD
I AM WHAT I AM
published by Diakonia Publishing in association with
Branches of the Vine Ministries
www.bovministries.net

For information:
DIAKONIA PUBLISHING
P.O. Box 9512
Greensboro, NC 27429
www.ephesians412.net

Acknowledgements

After honoring my Lord and Savior Jesus Christ for His inspiration to write this book, where does one begin to acknowledge and thank the many people that without their faithful support and contribution, you would not be reading these pages.

To Vicky Cheek, for her loyal friendship and contribution to the vision God had given me.

To David Gaadt, for his extraordinary artistic gift in taking the vision God had given me for the cover of this book.

To Laurie Nipper, a great friend and associate whose keen eye made what you're about to read that much better.

To Andrew Wommack, my mentor whose ministry ignited the calling of God in me.

To all my faithful ministry partners and supporters in Christ, without your efforts and listening ear, all this would be in vain.

Note About Scripture References

Although I teach primarily from the King James Version of the Bible, you will notice that I have attempted to make the text more "readable" by replacing the old English "thees" and "thous" with their modern-day equivalents. Additionally, some passages were reworded for the same purpose—to help the modern reader have a better understanding of the Scriptures without adding or taking anything away from the context of what was written or being taught.

Some traditionalists may not approve of this device, but I pray you will have grace in light of my desire to convey these truths to those who may not be familiar with the King James Version of the Bible. Finally, words contained in Scripture quotations that are capitalized, in bold, underlined, are used for emphasis only.

Come, you children, hearken unto me.
I will teach you the fear of the LORD.
— Psalm 34:11

CONTENTS

INTRODUCTION

But by the grace of God I am what I am.
1 Corinthians 15:10

Soon after being called into the ministry, the Lord inspired me to begin studying about our identity in Christ, and its importance to the believer. God revealed to me that His Church is in an identity crisis—a crisis that has been successful in keeping the saints of God from the fullness in relationship and from revealing who the Lord has called them to be; and consequently, has also rendered the church impotent and of marginal effect in the world today.

I WILL NOT BE NEGLIGENT TO PUT YOU ALWAYS IN REMEMBRANCE OF THESE THINGS.

2 Peter 1:9

This has occurred because many Christians have stumbled over what the word of God teaches concerning who they are in Christ. Because many have no idea who they are, they are living a life of vulnerability to the enemy that seeks to steal, kill, and destroy. As the Lord spoke in Hosea 4:6, *My people are destroyed for lack of knowledge*, many Christians are not experiencing the benefits of relationship with God. They are walking in fear instead of faith; depression instead of joy; sickness instead of divine health; and defeat instead of victory.

The primary reason for this is because they have been blinded from seeing who they are in Christ, in spite of what the Bible teaches. Thus, the purpose for this book *By the Grace of God, I Am What I*

Am—to point you back to what the word of God teaches about the most foundational of truths, answering the question: "Who am I?"

Despite many other issues and subjects pertaining to God's word, the Lord has always led me back to these foundational truths: Knowing and understanding the true meaning of eternal life (John 17:3); Knowing and comprehending His unconditional love and grace (Ephesians 3:18-19); Knowing and understanding the truth of the new birth (2 Corinthians 5:17) and our true identity in Christ (2 Corinthians 3:18). Since then, the Lord has given me a deeper revelation—not only of these truths, but also in their importance in breaking the strongholds of what has been traditionally taught in many churches. Before beginning, I'll repeat the prayer of the apostle Paul from Ephesians 1:17-20. Please read this carefully as this is God's desire for you in Christ Jesus:

MY PEOPLE ARE DESTROYED FOR LACK OF KNOWLEDGE.

Hosea 4:6

That the God of our Lord Jesus Christ, the Father of glory, may give unto you the spirit of wisdom and revelation in the knowledge of him. The eyes of your understanding being enlightened; that you may know what is the hope of his calling, and what the riches of the glory of his inheritance in the saints, and what is the exceeding greatness of his power toward us who believe, according to the working of his mighty power, which he wrought in Christ when he raised him from the dead, and set him at his own right hand in the heavenly places...

For the past several years, much of the body of Christ has concentrated its efforts on discovering "purpose" for their lives. While searching for "purpose" many have failed to realize the fact that in

I AM WHAT I AM

order to fully understand purpose, one must first know and embrace their identity. Then, once one knows what they were created to be, their purpose is revealed naturally, or albeit supernaturally. Because of this, the Lord led me to share the following parable.

There was once a hunter who came across an eagle's nest perched high upon a cliff. Inside the nest were three eggs left orphaned by their parents. Wanting to preserve the eagles, the hunter removed the nest and brought the eggs back to his farm in the country where he had several dozen chickens. After placing the eggs with one of his hens, several weeks went by and the eggs hatched.

Months went by and as the eagles grew, one eagle began hearing a voice inside, telling him that he was different from all the rest. He went to his brothers, the two other eagles, and told him what the voice had said. His brothers laughed at him and said that they were born chickens and they would remain chickens for the rest of their lives. They took him over to a large dusty mirror inside the hen house and the eagle looked at his distorted reflection. They said, "Our mother has feathers, you have feathers; our mother has wings, you have wings. Our mother is a chicken, you are a chicken."

"Their reasoning makes sense," the eagle said. "I seem to look like a chicken so I guess I am a chicken."

A year went by as the eagles lived as chickens. They pecked the ground for grain, hunted for worms and bugs, and most importantly, they never flew.

One day as the eagle wandered to the edge of the farm, he found

FOR TO BE CARNALLY MINDED IS DEATH; BUT TO BE SPIRITU-ALLY MINDED IS LIFE AND PEACE.

Romans 8:6

himself under a large tree. He heard a deep soft voice from above. "What are you doing here, young eagle?"

The eagle looked up to see a wise old owl perched on a branch. "I'm not an eagle; I'm a chicken, and I'm looking for bugs to eat."

The owl had a sad look on his face. Just then, his large wings began to open, and in a flash, the owl landed on the ground next to the eagle.

BUT THEY THAT WAIT UPON THE LORD SHALL RENEW THEIR STRENGTH; THEY SHALL MOUNT UP WITH WINGS AS EAGLES.

Isaiah 40:31

"Wow!" the eagle said. "I wish I could do that."

The owl sadly shook his head and removed a book from under his wings. He opened the book to a page and showed it to the eagle. The picture was of a large majestic bird, flying high in the sky.

"This is who you are," the owl said as he pointed at the picture. "You have allowed your circumstances and others to tell you that you were a chicken, when all along you were an eagle."

"But what about the mirror?" the eagle asked. "I have feathers and wings like all the other chickens. Why am I not a chicken like the rest of them?"

"Because the image you saw in the mirror was distorted. Yes, you possess the same physical qualities as a chicken like feathers and wings, but inside, you were created to be an eagle. Only until you can see who you really are will you be able to live the life God intended you to live." The owl held up the book. "Young eagle, this book tells us who God created us to be, and because you have seen your image inside, and I have told you the same, you must embrace it and fly."

I AM WHAT I AM

"Fly?" the eagle asked.

The owl smiled and nodded. "Yes, fly. All you have to do is believe that you are an eagle and you will fly as God created you to."

With a frightened look on his face, the eagle began to spread his wings.

"Don't be afraid, young eagle. Just believe."

With a tear in his eye, the young eagle believed and in an instant he was airborne, flying and soaring in the sky.

Many Christians today are in the same boat as that baby eagle. They come to Christ, but like the baby eagle, they are limited by what they see in the natural and know only what they've been taught. Their Christians "brothers" can only tell them that they're in essence just like the rest of the world. Only until they receive wisdom and truth do they look into the special mirror that tells them exactly who they are. This is what the Lord wants to accomplish through this book—to provide the body of Christ the truth that will set it free from the constraints placed upon it through religious tradition. When the apostle Paul proclaimed, "But by the grace of God, I am what I am," (1 Corinthians 15:10) he wasn't displaying a superiority complex, but rather, he was admitting that he had fully submitted to the grace of God, which made him who he was. It is my prayer that you, too, will be able to see who you really are in Christ, and by acknowledging these truths, you give glory to God. Amen.

WHO IS WISE, AND HE SHALL UNDERSTAND THESE THINGS? PRUDENT, AND HE SHALL KNOW THEM? FOR THE WAYS OF THE LORD ARE RIGHT, AND THE JUST SHALL WALK IN THEM; BUT THE TRANSGRESSORS SHALL FALL THEREIN.

Hosea 14:9

I will not be negligent to put you always in remembrance of these things, though you know them, and be established in the present truth. And I think it meet, as long as I am in this body, to stir you up by putting you in remembrance.

2 PETER 1:12-13

PART I

The Importance of Knowing Who You Are in Christ

For he received from God the Father honor and glory when there came such a voice to him from the excellent glory, This is my beloved Son, in whom I am well pleased. And this voice which came from heaven we heard when we were with him in the holy mount.

2 PETER 1:17-18

Apart from understanding eternal life and the extent by which we are reconciled to and have relationship with God, there is no more important truth than knowing who you are in Christ. This verse of scripture from 2 Peter (above) is so very powerful when trying to convey the importance of knowing exactly who we are in Christ. The Bible says that Jesus received honor and glory from the Father when the voice from heaven said, "This is my beloved Son, in whom I am well pleased."

In other words, the Lord Jesus received the honor and glory from God by believing who God said He was. Jesus knew that the word of God is the only authority by which you should know who you are and what God has destined for you. Our identity doesn't come from our parents, teachers, circumstances, or other people, or even from our own "self-image", but directly from God's mouth.

BUT LET HIM THAT GLORIES GLORY IN THIS, THAT HE UNDERSTANDS AND KNOWS ME, THAT I AM THE LORD WHO EXERCISES LOVING-KINDNESS, JUDGMENT, AND RIGHTEOUSNESS IN THE EARTH. FOR IN THESE THINGS I DELIGHT.

Jeremiah 9:24

That's why Jesus said, *It is written, Man shall not live by bread alone, but by every word that proceeds out of the mouth of God.* [Matthew 4: 4]

Therefore, if Jesus received honor and glory from God by believing who God said He was, then we should seek to learn what God has said about us in His word. As the Bible teaches, God's word is a mirror that reveals who we really are in Christ. Yet although people have read God's word, they are not walking in these truths. I hear what comes out of many Christians' mouths, and their words are in direct contradiction to what God has already established through His word. I even hear some preachers and other Christians identifying themselves as "sinners" and even the oxymoron "sinner saved by grace."

These ridiculous claims reflect the truth that many Christians have no idea who they are in Christ. The Bible says that *if any man be in Christ, he is a new creature. Old things are passed away; behold, all things are become new.* [2 Corinthians 5:17] This scripture teaches that we were sinners before receiving Christ, and after receiving Him, we became new creatures. If we were sinners before receiving Christ, and if the prevalent thinking were true, what new thing have we become—a new sinner? Even when we use common sense, it's easy to see how ridiculous this claim is. Instead of listening to what man has taught over the years, the Lord impressed upon me to begin searching the Bible for answers concerning who we are in Christ.

FOR CHRIST IS THE END OF THE LAW FOR RIGHTEOUS-NESS TO EVERYONE THAT BELIEVES.

Romans 10:4

1

A Solid Foundation

But let every man take heed how he builds thereupon. For other foundation can no man lay than that is laid, which is Jesus Christ.

1 Corinthians 3:10-11

IT IS WRITTEN, MAN SHALL NOT LIVE BY BREAD ALONE, BUT BY EVERY WORD THAT PROCEEDS OUT OF THE MOUTH OF GOD.

Matthew 4:4

The first important truth the Lord has shown me is that the foundation of our lives in Christ exists only when we know our true identities in Christ. Therefore, if we have not fully comprehended and believed what the Bible teaches concerning who we are in Christ, we have not established a strong foundation, but one that is weak and subject to being ruined when any storm arises.

This is what the Lord was teaching when He said, *Why do you call me, Lord, Lord, and do not the things which I say? Whosoever comes to me, and <u>hears my saying, and does them</u>, I will show you to whom he is like. He is like a man who built a house, and digged deep, and laid the foundation on a rock; and when the flood arose, the stream beat vehemently upon that house, and could not shake it; for it was founded upon a rock. But he that <u>hears, and does not</u>, is like a man that without a foundation built a house upon the earth; against which the stream did*

9

beat vehemently, and immediately it fell; and the ruin of that house was great. [Luke 6:46-49]

Many Christians haven't considered this passage to be a teaching about our identities in Christ, but it is. Jesus is teaching us about the difference between being a doer of the word and a hearer only. A person who both hears and acts upon the word of God has built his house upon a rock; while the hearer only has built his house upon earth or sand.

James taught the same principle in his epistle and described the person who hears the word only as having deceived themselves. *But be doers of the word, and not hearers only, deceiving your own selves. For if any be a hearer of the word, and not a doer, he is like unto a man beholding his natural face in a glass. For he beholds himself, and goes his way, and immediately forgets what manner of man he was.* [James 1:22-24]

As the Scripture says, one who hears the word only—and does not act upon it—has deceived himself in the same way we deceive ourselves by looking at our flesh—our natural faces—in a mirror and believe this is an accurate reflection of who we are. Furthermore, this deception is linked to forgetting what manner of man the word said he was, which indicates that the word of God tells us who we really are in Christ, but these truths are forgotten or perhaps more accurately, they are simply not believed.

The next verse in this passage proves this point. *But whoever looks into the perfect law of liberty, and continues therein, he being not a*

YOUR SINS ARE FORGIVEN YOU FOR HIS NAME'S SAKE.

1 John 2:12

forgetful hearer, but a doer of the work, this man shall be blessed in his deed. [James 1:25]

In his second letter to the Corinthian church, the apostle Paul also taught that we should see ourselves as being in Christ's image, using the same metaphor of looking into a mirror. *But we all, with open face beholding as in a glass* (mirror) *the glory of the Lord, are changed into the same image from glory to glory, even as by the Spirit of the Lord.* [2 Corinthians 3:18] As James wrote and as I will discuss later in chapter 10 "The True Mirror", the mirror James and Paul are referring to is the word of God.

Therefore, the person who does not fully understand what the word of God teaches concerning his or her identity in Christ, they have, as the Lord taught, built their house *without* a foundation (Luke 6:49). The apostle Paul wrote, *According to the grace of God which is given unto me, as a wise masterbuilder, I have laid the foundation, and another builds thereon. But let every man take heed how he builds thereupon. For other foundation can no man lay than that is laid, which is Jesus Christ.* [1 Corinthians 3:10-11]

Paul is teaching that through the gospel, he had laid the foundation of the truth in Christ as it relates to our identities. We see this because in verse 16 of this passage, after Paul explains what happens to what we have built upon the foundation (reward or burned), he connects the foundation to this truth: *Do you not know that you are the temple of God, and that the Spirit of God dwells in you? If any man defile the temple of God, him shall God destroy; for the temple of God is*

> DO YOU NOT KNOW THAT YOU ARE THE TEMPLE OF GOD, AND THAT THE SPIRIT OF GOD DWELLS IN YOU?
>
> *1 Cor. 3:16*

holy, which temple you are. Let no man deceive himself. If any man among you seem to be wise in this world, let him become a fool, that he may be wise. For the wisdom of this world is foolishness with God. For it is written, He takes the wise in their own craftiness. [1 Corinthians 3:16-19]

Once again, the Bible teaches that when a person fails to realize and walk (hear and do) in the truth of their identity in Christ, they have deceived themselves (see James 1:22). Defiling the temple of God isn't limited only to our actions, but we can defile the temple of God with words that are contrary to it. For example, as this passage teaches, you, as a Christian, are the temple of God; and the temple of God is holy; and therefore, you are holy. But if you consider yourself to be nothing but an old sinner, your words are defiling the temple of God.

The words of our Lord Jesus support this principle as well as it is written, *But those things which proceed out of the mouth come forth from the heart; and <u>they defile the man</u>.* [Matthew 15:18]

It is also written, *And the tongue is a fire, a world of iniquity; so is the tongue among our members, that it <u>defiles the whole body</u>, and sets on fire the course of nature; and it is set on fire of hell.* [James 3:6]

Our natural sense of logic tells us, "You're not holy. Every day you do something that amounts to sin. That's not what a holy person does." This logic is part of the wisdom of the world because it focuses entirely upon natural truths, while God's wisdom contained in the word of God speaks spiritual truths, which seem to be foolish

AND I MYSELF ALSO AM PERSUADED OF YOU, MY BRETHREN, THAT YOU ALSO ARE FULL OF GOODNESS, FILLED WITH ALL KNOWLEDGE, ABLE ALSO TO ADMONISH ONE ANOTHER.

Romans 15:14

I AM WHAT I AM

in comparison to worldly wisdom. Nevertheless, as it is written, *I will destroy the wisdom of the wise; and will bring to nothing the understanding of the prudent. God has chosen the foolish things of the world to confound the wise.* [1 Corinthians 1:19, 27]

Using natural wisdom, it may seem foolish to claim that you are holy, righteous, and full of goodness, but praise God that He desires that we become fools so that we may be wise according to God's wisdom.

As I will continue to teach throughout this book, the only foundation we can build our houses upon is the truth of our identities in Christ, as it is written, *Christ in you; the hope of glory.* [Colossians 1: 27] This is the mystery that had *been hid from ages and from generations, but now is made manifest to his saints* [Colossians 1:26] but unfortunately, many Christians have not opened their eyes to this truth, which explains why most Christians see themselves as ungodly sinners; live in defeat, sickness, and other rewards of the wicked. Only by understanding and walking in the truths of what the Bible teaches about who you are in Christ—in the spirit (not in the flesh) will you even begin to realize the extent of your inheritance in Christ Jesus.

In order to fully understand the importance of knowing who God says we are, we must first examine an incident where failure occurred as a result of not knowing who God says we are, and also, we will examine an incident where someone was victorious because they knew and believed who God said he was. These incidents are so strikingly similar that it would be difficult to misunderstand. One

IN WHOM YOU ALSO ARE BUILDED TOGETHER FOR A HABITA- TION OF GOD THROUGH THE SPIRIT.

Ephesians 2:22

doesn't have to turn very many pages in the Bible to find a failure in the bodies of Adam and Eve.

AS YOU
HAVE
THEREFORE
RECEIVED
CHRIST
JESUS THE
LORD, SO
WALK IN
HIM.

Colossians 2:6

The Fall of Adam and Eve

But I fear, lest by any means, as the serpent beguiled Eve through his subtlety, so your minds should be corrupted from the simplicity that is in Christ.

2 CORINTHIANS 11:3

Most Christians have understood that as a result of Adam and Eve's sin in the garden, the entire human race was catapulted into the bondage of sin and separation from the life of God. While this truth is understood by most, the reasons they fell are not completely understood because if they were, we would be seeing the glory of God being manifested in and through His children in a greater way than we are today. I'll pose this question: Why did Adam and Eve fall into sin?

The drugstore answer is almost always, "Because Eve was deceived by the devil and when she and Adam ate the fruit of the tree of knowledge of good and evil, they had rebelled against God."

For lack of time and space, I cannot delve into all the possible answers, but this answer, while correct, reveals only a superficial understanding of why Adam and Eve fell. In order to get to the truth, one must do as Jesus said, *Launch out into the deep and let down your nets for a draught.* [Luke 5:4] In each case, we will first examine what God had said, and then look at the subsequent temptation from the devil.

So God created man in his own image, in the image of God he created him; male and female he created them. And God blessed them, and God said unto them, Be fruitful, and multiply, and replenish the earth, and subdue it. And have dominion over the fish of the sea, and over the fowl of the air, and over every living thing that moves upon the earth. [Genesis 1:27-28]

It Bears Repeating

So God created man in his own image, in the image of God he created him; male and female he created them.

God created man in His own image. It wasn't enough to say it once, but the writer Moses, being inspired by the Spirit of God, repeated this truth, *in the image of God he created him: male and female he created them.* It's important to understand when the Bible repeats itself, this is a clue to you that you really should take heed to what it is saying. When Jesus said, *Truly, truly I say to you, Except a man be born again, he cannot see the kingdom of God.* [John 3:3] the Lord was stressing this point by repeating not only the fact that He was telling the truth, but in that He repeated the same words in verse 5.

The apostle Paul repeated himself at times as well. In his letter

WHAT IS MAN, THAT YOU ARE MINDFUL OF HIM? AND THE SON OF MAN, THAT YOU VISIT HIM?

Psalm 8:4

to the Philippian church, Paul used the word "rejoice" ten (10) times. *Rejoice in the Lord always. And again I say, Rejoice.* [Philippians 4:4]

Blessed With Power and Authority

And God blessed them, and God said unto them, Be fruitful, and multiply, and replenish the earth, and subdue it. And have dominion over the fish of the sea, and over the fowl of the air, and over every living thing that moves upon the earth.

After creating Adam and Eve, God blessed them with His word and with power and authority over all the earth. I know some of you may struggle with what I'm about say, but God had made Adam and Eve gods over the earth. They weren't God with a big G, but gods with a small g, in that God had created them to be godly beings, and had also given them complete power and authority over everything in the earth. So, in truth, God is God; and Adam and Eve were, as images of God, gods of the earth, as it written, *You have crowned him with glory and honor, and did set him over the works of your hands. You have put all things in subjection under his feet.* [Hebrews 2:7-8; Psalm 8:5-6] Let us also remember that when God blessed them, Adam and Eve had not yet sinned, and were perfect.

When we examine God's word, we find, in two places, references to men being "gods". The Lord Jesus quoted Psalm 82:6 when He said, *Is it not written in your law, I said, You are gods? If he called them gods, unto whom the word of God came, and the scripture cannot be broken, do you say of him, whom the Father has sanctified, and sent*

> BLESSED IS THE MAN THAT TRUSTS IN THE LORD, AND WHOSE HOPE THE LORD IS.
>
> *Jeremiah 17:7*

into the world, You blaspheme, because I said, I am the Son of God? [John 10:34-36]

Psalm 82:6 says: *I have said, You are gods, and all of you are children of the most High.*

Understanding the words of Jesus and the quote from Psalms, we can rightly conclude that since we are children of God, and we are to whom the word of God came, this scripture applied to Adam and Eve as well.

THERE HAS NO TEMP-TATION TAKEN YOU BUT SUCH AS IS COMMON TO MAN. BUT GOD IS FAITHFUL...

1 Cor. 10:13

The Temptation

Now the serpent was more subtle than any beast of the field which the LORD God had made. And he said unto the woman, Yea, has God said, You shall not eat of every tree of the garden?

And the woman said unto the serpent, We may eat of the fruit of the trees of the garden. But of the fruit of the tree which is in the midst of the garden, God has said, You shall not eat of it, neither shall you touch it, lest you die.

And the serpent said unto the woman, You shall not surely die. For God does know that in the day you eat thereof, then your eyes shall be opened, and you shall be as gods, knowing good and evil.

And when the woman saw that the tree was good for food, and that it was pleasant to the eyes, and a tree to be desired to make one wise, she took of the fruit thereof, and did eat, and gave also to her husband with her; and he did eat. [Genesis 3:1-6]

I AM WHAT I AM

Their First Mistake—Doubting God's Word

While many people have criticized Eve for engaging in a conversation with the serpent, I believe the Bible reveals that her reply was according to what the Bible teaches. Her answer was similar to that of Jesus when tempted in the wilderness. She answered with God's word: *God has said, You shall not eat of it, neither shall you touch it, lest you die.* Here the serpent was attacking God's integrity—in that God had deceived them (*You shall not surely die*) and had blinded them from knowing the "real" truth. How often does this come up in the world today? How often do people say that God's word doesn't work—that God doesn't desire you to be healed in your body and mind—that God doesn't want you to be prosperous?

Eve's first mistake was allowing the serpent to cause her to doubt God's word concerning the consequences of disobedience; then following up with the inference that God was withholding something from them. If these verses reflect the sequence of events, which I believe they do, then it was Eve's doubt of God's word that led her to look upon the tree, causing her to consider what the serpent had said. Read the verses again. It was only after the serpent questioned God's word that Eve looked upon the tree. Before the temptation, had Eve ever considered the desirability of the fruit? I doubt she had because the scripture infers that this was the first time Eve had ever noticed it in this way. There is no question that she and Adam had seen the tree before since it had been placed in the midst of the garden, but it was like she said, "Wow, I never noticed how appeal-

YOUR WORD HAVE I HID IN MY HEART, THAT I MIGHT NOT SIN AGAINST YOU.

Psalm 119:11

19

ing this fruit looks!" Then, as the Scripture teaches in James 1:14, she was *drawn away of her own lust.*

Satan was trying to exalt something against the knowledge of God, and as the Scripture teaches, it should have been cast down and/or taken captive to the obedience of God's word (2 Corinthians 10:3-5).

BE NOT WISE IN YOUR OWN EYES. FEAR THE LORD, AND DEPART FROM EVIL.

Proverbs 3:7

What we can learn is that the serpent caused Eve to do something she probably had never done, which was to consider her own self. The fruit was *good for food, pleasant to the eyes,* and *desirable to make one wise.* Selfishness is the root of all sin, and by casting doubt on God's word, the serpent induced Eve to esteem her own needs over the word of God. Once she looked to her own needs, she had fallen into the trap that always leads to destruction. If the devil can get you to doubt God's word, then he's on the way of leading you into sin. Doubt caused Eve to hesitate and consider the serpent's lies when she could (and should) have completely trusted in God's word and countered again with what God had said.

I want to add a parenthetical point to this verse if I may, because I think it reveals a lot about the person of Adam. In Genesis 2:16-17 we read: *And the LORD God commanded the man, saying, Of every tree of the garden you may freely eat. But of the tree of the knowledge of good and evil, you shall not eat of it. For in the day that you eat thereof you shall surely die.*

The next verse gives account to the formation of the woman, and we can rightly conclude that since Eve was not present to hear

God's command (and scripture does not tell us that God had given the command directly to her) Adam must have conveyed this command to his wife. We can see from Eve's reply to the serpent that Adam had added to God's command by saying that she could not even touch the fruit of the tree. I liken this "addition" to a parent warning his child against playing with a fragile item. Not only should they not "play" with the item, but they should not even "touch" it.

We can look at Adam's additional warning as either a "stroke of divine wisdom" or a manifestation of pride, which eventually led to his downfall. Ask yourself these questions: Did Adam need to add to God's command? Did he know her better than God? Although we see that this additional warning was not effective in keeping Eve from succumbing to the temptation, we do learn another lesson from it, in that the greater the law of prohibition, the greater the desire to do what is prohibited. Perhaps, Adam's additional warning served as a seed of unbelief in what God had told him, which may have been what eventually lured Eve into partaking of the fruit. This truth reveals the effects of legalism and how the law will actually make you lust for sin. Paul's letters to the Galatians and Colossians clearly explain this issue.

Their Second Mistake—Not Knowing Who They Were

Similar to the temptation of Jesus, the devil did not stop after one attempt. After her reply, the serpent turned God's word around and attacked who God had said she was. *And the serpent said unto the*

> EVERY WORD OF GOD IS PURE. HE IS A SHIELD UNTO THEM THAT PUT THEIR TRUST IN HIM. ADD NOT UNTO HIS WORDS, LEST HE REPROVE YOU, AND YOU BE FOUND A LIAR.
>
> *Proverbs 30:5-6*

woman, You shall not surely die. For God does know that in the day you eat thereof, then your eyes shall be opened, and <u>you shall be as gods, knowing good and evil.</u>

In addition to calling God a liar, the serpent questioned her identity, or who God had said she was, which is the very root of the problem we face today: Doubting what God has said, and not knowing who God says you are. Eve's reply should have been this: "God has said that I was created in the image of God and He has blessed me and given me authority and dominion over the earth. Now, I take authority over you and command you to leave!"

However, we know that she didn't say anything—at least no further response is recorded—and we see that their transgression propelled the entire human race into the bondage of the devil, for which the Lord Jesus had to pay the ransom to make us free.

If you recall the previous passage from Genesis 1, God had already made Adam and Eve "gods" over the earth. Therefore, they had no need to be "like gods" because they had been created in the image of God. Now we clearly see the consequences of not knowing who we really are.

GOD IS NOT A MAN THAT HE SHOULD LIE, NEITHER THE SON OF MAN THAT HE SHOULD REPENT. HAS HE SAID, AND SHALL HE NOT DO IT? OR HAS HE SPOKEN, AND SHALL HE NOT MAKE IT GOOD?

Numbers 23:19

3
The Victory of Jesus

For he received from God the Father honor and glory, when there came such a voice to him from the excellent glory, This is my beloved Son, in whom I am well pleased.

2 PETER 1:17

Now that we've learned from Adam and Eve's mistakes, we can turn to the Lord Jesus and His experience in the wilderness to see how and why He was victorious over temptation. I reiterate the point that the two incidents are so strikingly similar, that we cannot help learning from them.

First, let us re-affirm the humanity of Jesus, in that not only is He fully God, but He is also fully man. The Bible speaks of His humanity in numerous places, but I will cite three verses of scripture that support this truth.

- *But we see Jesus, who was made a little lower than the angels for the suffering of death, crowned with glory and honor; that he by the grace of God should taste death for every man.* [Hebrews 2:9]
- *Seeing then that we have a great high priest, that is passed into*

the heavens, Jesus the Son of God, let us hold fast our profession. For we have not a high priest which cannot be touched with the feeling of our infirmities; but was in all points tempted like as we are, yet without sin. [Hebrews 4:14-15]

- *Let this mind be in you, which was also in Christ Jesus, who, being in the form of God, thought it not robbery to be equal with God. But made himself of no reputation, and took upon him the form of a servant, and was made in the likeness of men. And being found in fashion as a man, he humbled himself, and became obedient unto death, even the death of the cross.* [Philippians 2:5-8]

It is so very important for us to understand that Jesus was found to be a man. Although being the eternal God, He became a man so that He could redeem mankind by His own sacrifice. While His body was sinless, it was flesh like ours, and consequently, He was still subject to the natural things we all experience (hunger, sleep, temptation, etc.).

Similar to us, Jesus had to grow in wisdom and stature (Luke 2:52). When Jesus was born, His physical mind did not know all things. He had to be taught how to walk, talk, eat, and so on. Furthermore, Jesus had to learn through revelation that He was the Son of God, and accept this truth by faith. Most people have failed to comprehend this truth—that Jesus the man, had to walk by faith in who He was—just as we have to walk by faith in the knowledge of who we are in Christ. I cannot stress this enough. Jesus had to walk

GREAT IS THE MYSTERY OF GODLINESS: GOD WAS MANIFEST IN THE FLESH, JUSTIFIED IN THE SPIRIT, SEEN OF ANGELS, PREACHED UNTO THE GENTILES, BELIEVED ON IN THE WORLD, RECEIVED UP INTO GLORY.

1 Timothy 3:16

I AM WHAT I AM

by faith. We have been blinded from this truth because the majority of our visual perceptions of Jesus depict Him with a halo around His head, or some other supernatural effect that represents His divinity, but at the same time prevents us from truly identifying with His humanity.

Therein lies the problem—that although God, through Jesus, is able to identify and relate to our weaknesses (Hebrews 4:14-15) we have failed to completely identify ourselves with the humanity of Jesus—that He came to be our example in faith, love, life, and power. And I know many people may criticize this, thinking I'm trying to bring God down to our human level. Rather, I'm trying to bring light of what the word of God teaches—that He wants us to look higher and realize our place in Christ as it is written, *But God, who is rich in mercy, for his great love wherewith he loved us, even when we were dead in sins, has quickened us together with Christ (by grace you are saved) and has raised us up together, and made us sit together in heavenly places in Christ Jesus.* [Ephesians 2:4-6]

Through an understanding of the humanity of Jesus, and how He had to walk by faith in who He was, we can apply His victory over temptation to our own lives.

And Jesus, when he was baptized, went up immediately out of the water, and lo, the heavens were opened to him, and he saw the Spirit of God descending like a dove, and lighting upon him. And lo, a voice from heaven, saying, This is my beloved Son, in whom I am well pleased. Then Jesus was led up of the Spirit into the wilderness to be tempted of the devil. And when he had fasted forty days and forty nights, he was

AND HAVING SPOILED PRINCI-PALITIES AND POWERS, HE MADE A SHOW OF THEM OPENLY, TRIUMPH-ING OVER THEM IN IT.

Colossians 2:15

By the Grace of God

afterward hungry.

And when the tempter came to him, he said, If you are the Son of God, command that these stones be made bread.

But he answered and said, It is written, Man shall not live by bread alone, but by every word that proceeds out of the mouth of God.

Then the devil took him up into the holy city, and set him on a pinnacle of the temple, and said to him, If you are the Son of God, cast yourself down; for it is written, He shall give his angels charge concerning you. And in their hands they shall bear you up, lest at any time you dash your foot against a stone.

Jesus said to him, It is written again, You shall not tempt the Lord your God.

Again, the devil took him up into an exceeding high mountain, and showed him all the kingdoms of the world, and the glory of them, and said to him, All these things I will give to you, if you will fall down and worship me.

Then Jesus said to him, Get from here, Satan. For it is written, You shall worship the Lord your God, and him only shall you serve.

Then the devil left him, and behold, angels came and ministered to him. [Matthew 3:16-4:11]

IN THAT DAY SHALL THE LORD OF HOSTS BE FOR A CROWN OF GLORY, AND FOR A DIADEM OF BEAUTY, UNTO THE RESIDUE OF HIS PEOPLE.

Isaiah 28:5

Honor and Glory From the Father

After being baptized, Jesus came out of the water and received honor and glory from the Father when a voice came from heaven saying, *This is my beloved Son, in whom I am well pleased.* The glory and

26

honor Jesus had received was by knowing who He was—the Son of God—not because of His own revelation, but because God had said it. Let's recall the verse from 2 Peter 1:17-18: *For he received from God the Father honor and glory when there came such a voice to him from the excellent glory, This is my beloved Son, in whom I am well pleased. And this voice which came from heaven we heard when we were with him in the holy mount.*

We compare this event to Creation and God's word that said Adam and Eve were created in the image of God. Adam and Eve had received the same glory and honor from God when He blessed them and gave them dominion over everything in the earth. Let me repeat this: Jesus received glory and honor from the Father when He said, *This is my beloved Son, in whom I am well pleased.*

We will see later on in this book that not only does God call us *sons of God* (John 1:12; 1 John 3:2) and that we are *accepted* (or highly favored) *in the beloved* (Ephesians 1:6; 2 Corinthians 5:9) but that we are to His *praise, honor and glory* (Romans 2:7, 10; Ephesians 1:12). According to Hebrews 2:7 and Psalm 8:5, we have been *crowned with glory and honor.*

I want to mention one point about us being pleasing to God. God said, "This is my beloved Son, in whom I am well pleased." The phrase *in whom* is vital because when we consider someone being pleasing to us, we always phrase it this way, "I am pleased *with* you—not pleased *in* you." And while I'm certain that God was well pleased *with* Jesus, but this passage says that God was pleased *in Him*, which

AND HE THAT SENT ME IS WITH ME. THE FATHER HAS NOT LEFT ME ALONE; FOR I DO ALWAYS THOSE THINGS THAT PLEASE HIM.

John 8:29

refes to whosoever is *in Christ*. That's us, my brothers and sisters, which correlates perfectly with Romans 8:8-9 that says *So then they that are in the flesh cannot please God. But you are not in the flesh, but in the Spirit, if so be that the Spirit of God dwells in you. Now if any man have not the Spirit of Christ, he is none of his.* Additionally, this fits perfectly with Hebrews 11:6 that says, *But without faith it is impossible to please him...*

Therefore, we see that God's pleasure with us is based entirely upon your position in Christ, whom you received by faith; and as long as you remain in faith, you will abide in Christ and will be well pleasing to God. The revelation of this one truth set me free from trying to perform for God in order to be pleasing to Him. My prayer is that it will set you free as well.

FOR THIS PURPOSE WAS THE SON OF GOD MANIFESTED, THAT HE MIGHT DESTROY THE WORKS OF THE DEVIL.

1 John 3:8

Satan's First Attack

Then Jesus was led up of the Spirit into the wilderness to be tempted of the devil. And when he had fasted forty days and forty nights, he was afterward hungry.

And when the tempter came to him, he said, If you are the Son of God, command that these stones be made bread.

But he answered and said, It is written, Man shall not live by bread alone, but by every word that proceeds out of the mouth of God.

As you should see, the devil's strategy hasn't changed since the garden. The first words out of the devil's mouth, having heard what the Father had said to Jesus, (*This is my beloved Son, in whom I am*

I AM WHAT I AM

well pleased) the devil tried to get Jesus to doubt God's word by attacking who God said Jesus was. The devil said, *IF you are the Son of God, command that these stones be made bread.* While the serpent appealed to Eve's desires for food first, and then attacked her identity, he attacked the identity of Jesus before appealing to His desire for food.

You know, we give the devil way too much credit for being so cunning. Granted, he is a master liar, but his strategy hasn't changed one bit since the garden. Why? Because this strategy has worked on man so often and with such ease, that the devil hasn't been forced to try anything different.

Because the devil is so subtle and so that you may not miss this point, by saying, "If you are the Son of God" he was casting doubt in God's word concerning who Jesus was. The devil didn't say, "Because you are the Son of God..." As with Eve, Jesus' first response was with God's word, quoting from Deuteronomy 8:3: *It is written,* (or God has said) *Man shall not live by bread alone, but by every word that proceeds out of the mouth of God.*

Here, Jesus went a step further than Eve by re-affirming that God's word is sole and final authority in terms of both our needs and identity. However, Satan didn't stop there.

Satan's Second Attack

Then the devil took him up into the holy city, and set him on a pinnacle

BUT BE DOERS OF THE WORD, AND NOT HEARERS ONLY, DECEIVING YOUR OWN SELVES.

James 1:22

of the temple, and said to him, If you are the Son of God, cast yourself down; for it is written, He shall give his angels charge concerning you. And in their hands they shall bear you up, lest at any time you dash your foot against a stone.

Jesus said to him, It is written again, You shall not tempt the Lord your God.

Again, the devil tried to cast doubt in the mind of Jesus concerning who He was (*If you are the Son of God*), but this time, the devil also attacked Him with pride. Similar to his strategy with Eve, the devil tried to use the word of God against Jesus by quoting (or rather mis-quoting) from Psalm 91:11-12: *For he shall give his angels charge over you, to keep you in all your ways. They shall bear you up in their hands, lest you dash your foot against a stone.* The devil also added the phrase "at any time" giving place to the notion that God's power was available to Jesus, even if He were outside of God's will.

This point is so very important for you to understand. The devil will use the word of God against you—to bring condemnation, guilt, shame, hopelessness, pride, unbelief, and even (as in the case of Adam and Eve) attempt to lead you into sin. This is why I must say that the devil has inspired the doctrine that claims that we are still sinners after receiving the gift of righteousness that is given by God through Jesus Christ. I don't care what your pastor says; I don't care what some prominent evangelists or theologians say; I am concerned only by what God has said through His word. This reminds me of a very profound statement by the Lord Jesus: *How can you believe, which receive honor one of another, and seek not the honor that comes from God only?* [John 5:44]

Once again, the Lord responded with the sword of the Spirit— the word of God—by saying, *It is written again, You shall not tempt the Lord your God.* While Eve remained silent after the second attack, the Lord Jesus continued wielding the sword. Also notice that Jesus did not correct the devil's mis-statement of God's word—rather, He used the word correctly to counter this perversion.

FINALLY, MY BRETHREN, BE STRONG IN THE LORD AND IN THE POWER OF HIS MIGHT...

Ephesians 6:10

Satan's Third Attack

Again, the devil took him up into an exceeding high mountain, and showed him all the kingdoms of the world, and the glory of them, and said to him, All these things I will give to you, if you will fall down and worship me.

Then Jesus said to him, Get from here, Satan. For it is written, You shall worship the Lord your God, and him only shall you serve.

Then the devil left him, and behold, angels came and ministered to him.

The results of the second attack on Jesus left the devil in somewhat of a dilemma. He couldn't get Jesus to doubt who He was, to doubt God's word and be trapped by the misuse of God's word. Consequently, the devil was forced to take a chance that Jesus could be defeated by the lure of riches and power at the expense of forsaking His Father. He was wrong and Jesus slashed the sword once again, *For it is written, You shall worship the Lord God, and him only shall you serve.*

A key verse in this account is *Then the devil left him, and behold angels came and ministered to him.* The lesson learned here is this: that the devil will be persistent, but if you stand strongly on the word of God and are not moved from what God has said, and who God has said you are, the devil will eventually depart from you for a time.

In addition to the direct attacks on His identity by Satan, the devil used people to continue these attacks throughout the Lord's ministry. As I said before, Jesus had to walk by faith in who He was in order to fulfill His calling.

Most Christians are familiar with Matthew 16 when the Lord had asked the disciples who people had said Jesus was. Peter stood and proclaimed, *You are the Christ, the Son of the living God.* [Matthew 16:16]

Immediately after this revelation from God, the devil used Peter to attack the Lord's identity and calling. Many Christians haven't considered Peter's rebuke of Jesus, *Be it far from you, Lord. This shall not be unto you* [Matthew 16:22] as an attempt by the devil to thwart the Lord's faith. We must remember that Jesus could have easily succumbed to this temptation, as like us, He certainly didn't want to die on the cross. However, by not dying on the cross, Jesus, while continuing to live on earth, would not have fulfilled His calling by God.

The Pharisees also constantly questioned who Jesus was, and questioned by what authority did He have in doing the things He

I AM WHAT I AM

did. These were all attempts by the devil to try to get Jesus to doubt who He was.

While Jesus was dying on the cross, the devil continued his attacks, trying to the very end to tempt Jesus into doing something outside the will of God. Onlookers railed Him saying, *If you are the Son of God, come down from the cross. Likewise also the chief priests mocking him, with the scribes and elders said, He saved others; himself he cannot save. If he is the King of Israel, let him now come down from the cross, and we will believe him.* [Matthew 27:40-42]

Satan's Strategy

As you have seen through the temptations of Adam and Eve, and also with Jesus, the devil's primary strategy consists of questioning God's word, especially in regard to who you are in God's eyes. I cannot stress this enough. Scripture tells us plainly of these truths, yet much of the body of Christ is continuing to believe the devil's lies and refer to themselves as "sinners", "worms", etc. Look at the temptations again. The devil was trying to cast doubt as to who Jesus was. He said, "If you are the Son of God," not "Because you are the Son of God."

The devil's strategy hasn't changed, nor will it because his only weapons are deception and temptation. When you refer to yourself as nothing but "an old sinner saved by grace" you are surrendering the fight before it even begins. This is why I make such a bold claim that Satan is behind the predominant thinking of many Christians

BE SOBER, BE VIGILANT; BECAUSE YOUR ADVERSARY THE DEVIL, AS A ROARING LION, WALKS ABOUT, SEEKING WHOM HE MAY DEVOUR.

1 Peter 5:8

when they see themselves as sinners.

It's funny, that before we received Christ, many of us would have never claimed to be a "sinner". But now that we have been made righteous by the sacrifice of Jesus, we take this brand and wear it proudly. We have allowed the devil to blind us before Christ, and once our eyes have been opened, we allow him to blind us to the truth of what happened when we were born again. This may sound brutal, but I've never won any awards for subtlety. If you have been born again and still see and refer to yourself as a sinner, then you are blind and deceived. In the section of this book entitled "The True Mirror" I will confirm this truth.

Three Tools of Temptation

The devil uses three tools of temptation and deception against people. All three of these were used both in the garden with Eve and against the Lord Jesus in the wilderness. All these are used after the devil attempts to cast doubt in God's word. The Bible supports this in the following verse of scripture: *For all that is in the world, the lust of the flesh, and the lust of the eyes, and the pride of life, is not of the Father, but is of the world.* [1 John 1:16] The devil's strategy is to:

- Entice you with desires of the flesh
- Entice you with things that are pleasing to the eyes
- Entice you by appealing to the pride of life

You can see that the following passage contains three temptations that, after doubting God's word, led Adam and Eve into sin.

FOR WHATSOEVER THINGS WERE WRITTEN AFORETIME WERE WRITTEN FOR OUR LEARNING, THAT WE THROUGH PATIENCE AND COMFORT OF THE SCRIPTURES MIGHT HAVE HOPE.

Romans 15:4

I AM WHAT I AM

And when the woman saw that the tree was good for food (lust of the flesh), *and that it was pleasant to the eyes* (lust of the eyes), *and a tree to be desired to make one wise* (the pride of life), *she took of the fruit thereof, and did eat, and gave also to her husband with her; and he did eat.*

In the temptation of Jesus, the devil presented these things in a slightly different package, but nonetheless, they were present: *Command that these stones be made bread* (lust of the flesh). *Cast yourself down...* (pride of life) and *showed him the kingdoms of the world, and the glory of them...* (lust of the eyes).

Now that you have an understanding of the importance of knowing who you are in Christ, let us explore what the Bible says concerning who we really are in Christ.

NOW WE HAVE RECEIVED, NOT THE SPIRIT OF THE WORLD, BUT THE SPIRIT WHICH IS OF GOD; THAT WE MIGHT KNOW THE THINGS THAT ARE FREELY GIVEN TO US OF GOD. *1 Cor. 2:12*

O how i love your law! It is my meditation all the day.

You through your commandments have made me wiser than my enemies. For they are ever with me.

I have more understanding than all my teachers. For your testimonies are my meditation.

I understand more than the ancients, because I keep your precepts.

I have refrained my feet from every evil way, that I might keep your word.

I have not departed from your judgments. For you have taught me.

How sweet are your words unto my taste! Yea, sweeter than honey to my mouth!

Through your precepts I get understanding. Therefore I hate every false way.

~Psalm 119:97-104

PART II

The New Creature

And the LORD said unto Joshua, This day have I rolled away the reproach of Egypt from off you…

JOSHUA 5:9

WHO IS A GOD LIKE UNTO YOU, THAT PARDONS INIQUITY, AND PASSES BY THE TRANSGRESSION OF THE REMNANT OF HIS HERITAGE? HE RETAINS NOT HIS ANGER FOR EVER, BECAUSE HE DELIGHTS IN MERCY. HE WILL TURN AGAIN, HE WILL HAVE COMPASSION UPON US; HE WILL SUBDUE OUR INIQUITIES; AND YOU WILL CAST ALL THEIR SINS INTO THE DEPTHS OF THE SEA. YOU WILL PERFORM THE TRUTH TO JACOB, AND THE MERCY TO ABRAHAM, WHICH YOU HAVE SWORN UNTO OUR FATHERS FROM THE DAYS OF OLD.

~Micah 7:18-20

YET IT PLEASED THE LORD TO BRUISE HIM; HE HAS PUT HIM TO GRIEF. WHEN YOU SHALL MAKE HIS SOUL AN OFFERING FOR SIN, HE SHALL SEE HIS SEED, HE SHALL PROLONG HIS DAYS, AND THE PLEASURE OF THE LORD SHALL PROSPER IN HIS HAND. HE SHALL SEE OF THE TRAVAIL OF HIS SOUL, AND SHALL BE SATISFIED. BY HIS KNOWLEDGE SHALL MY RIGHTEOUS SERVANT JUSTIFY MANY; FOR HE SHALL BEAR THEIR INIQUITIES. THEREFORE WILL I DIVIDE HIM A PORTION WITH THE GREAT, AND HE SHALL DIVIDE THE SPOIL WITH THE STRONG; BECAUSE HE HAS POURED OUT HIS SOUL UNTO DEATH. AND HE WAS NUMBERED WITH THE TRANSGRESSORS; AND HE BORE THE SIN OF MANY, AND MADE INTERCESSION FOR THE TRANSGRESSORS.

~Isaiah 53:10-12

The New Birth in Christ

Therefore if any man be in Christ, he is a new creature. Old things are passed away; behold, all things are become new.

2 CORINTHIANS 5: 17

Although this verse from 2 Corinthians 5 is about as straightforward as any can get, many people do not yet understand the truth of the new creature completely. At some point in their lives, they heard the gospel and received the gift of salvation that comes only through faith in Jesus Christ.

Here's a typical scenario. Many were told that they were new creatures in Christ, and that their lives would be different from then on, but they did not see or feel any significant change in their behavior. As time goes by, and without a noticeable change, they begin to wonder if they were truly saved. Their fellow church members tell them that as soon as they begin obeying God's commandments, they will see a noticeable change in their life. Consequently, this person becomes consumed with holiness and obeying the commandments of God, only to discover that the change in his life was not for the better, but for the worse. Not only has he not been able to cease from sin, but the desire for sin has grown.

Then, he goes to his pastor and asks for godly counsel, only to be told that even after being born again, he is still a sinner because he still commits sin. The man is confused because when he received Christ, he had to admit that he was a sinner, and that afterward, he was a new creature. The pastor's answer was that now he was a "sinner walking daily and continuously in the saving grace of God." Then perhaps the man is told that each time he commits a sin, he must "come to the throne of grace" and ask for forgiveness of his sins because sin separated him from God, and in order to be "right" with God, one must confess your sins and ask for forgiveness. Otherwise, if he died he would not be saved.

Consequently, the man becomes mired in the bondage of living according to his own obedience to God's law and will never truly know whether he is in "right standing" with God. Because of this way of thinking, he will live a life at the whim of the devil, who will bring condemnation on him every time he misses the mark. And even worse, the man will think that God is the one condemning him, or as it is commonly said, "The Lord is convicting me of sin."

The sad part of this picture is that a vast majority of Christians have this very same mindset. They see themselves in the flesh—as nothing but an "old sinner saved by grace"—instead of looking into God's word to find the truth. God never intended for you to take the burden of sin upon yourself. It is true that sin separates a person

O FOOLISH GALATIANS, WHO HAS BEWITCHED YOU, THAT YOU SHOULD NOT OBEY THE TRUTH, BEFORE WHOSE EYES JESUS CHRIST HAS BEEN EVIDENTLY SET FORTH, CRUCIFIED AMONG YOU?

Galatians 3:1

I AM WHAT I AM

from intimate relationship with God, but *sin* in this case is a noun—not a verb—indicating that the sinful nature is what prevented you from having this intimate relationship with God. This is why Jesus came and died—so that He would restore the relationship that was lost as a result of Adam and Eve's transgression. Jesus said, *For the Son of man is come to save that which was lost.* [Matthew 18:11]

It just so happened that sin was what stood between God and man. Therefore, Jesus had to take the sins of the world upon Himself while dying on the cross. Isaiah 53:4-5 says, *Surely he has borne our griefs and carried our sorrows. Yet we did esteem him stricken, smitten of God, and afflicted. But he was wounded for our transgressions; he was bruised for iniquities; the chastisement of our peace was upon him; and with his stripes we are healed.*

Jesus said it this way: *Come unto me, all you that labor and are heavy laden, and I will give you rest. Take my yoke upon you; for I am meek and lowly in heart. And you shall find rest unto your souls. For my yoke is easy, and my burden light.* [Matthew 11:28-30]

For the Father judges no man, but has committed all judgment unto the Son, that all men should honor the Son, even as they honor the Father. He that honors not the Son honors not the Father which has sent him. [John 5:22-23]

Verse 18 from 2 Corinthians 5 confirms the truth of the new creature. Verse 17 says that *all things have become new,* and verse 18 says that *all things are of God, who has reconciled us to himself by Jesus Christ, and has given to us the ministry of reconciliation.*

> AND THIS IS LIFE ETERNAL, THAT THEY MIGHT KNOW YOU THE ONLY TRUE GOD, AND JESUS CHRIST, WHOM YOU HAVE SENT.
>
> *John 17:3*

41

We can make the conclusion that the "all things are of God" refers to the new creature, because we also know that before we received Christ, we were, by nature, children of wrath (Ephesians 2:3). In Christ, we have been given a new nature, which is of God. My brothers and sisters, God and the devil cannot occupy the same space. Either you have the nature of God through the regenerating and washing of the Spirit of God, or you still have the nature of the devil. The Bible makes a clear distinction of our nature and position prior to being born again, and the truth of the new creature as it is written, (God) *who has delivered us from the power of darkness, and has translated us into the kingdom of his dear Son.* [Colossians 1:13]

This passage is teaching that we have been delivered (past tense) from the power of sin and the law—the sinful nature that compelled us to violate God's law—and has translated (past tense) or supernaturally transferred us into the kingdom of His Son.

Other Christians have been taught that the Lord gets angry or displeased when we blow it. How many of you, after committing a sin, thinking that God is mad at you, will try to hide or stay away from God until He cools down? Then, after a few hours or days, you come back to Him and your conscience is restored. This attitude is a catastrophe waiting to happen.

Brothers and sisters, this is a vital truth and I pray you have ears to hear. Jesus suffered the pain of separation from God due to sin so you would not have to suffer. By submitting to condemnation and separating yourself from God, you are in essence, claiming that Jesus

FOR THIS IS AS THE WATERS OF NOAH UNTO ME: FOR AS I HAVE SWORN THAT THE WATERS OF NOAH SHOULD NO MORE GO OVER THE EARTH; SO HAVE I SWORN THAT I WOULD NOT BE ANGRY WITH YOU, NOR REBUKE YOU.

Isaiah 54:9

I AM WHAT I AM

didn't suffer enough for you—that you too must also make an atonement for sin. This is why we have God's grace—not to minimize sin, but to magnify and exalt what Jesus did for us on the cross.

When you commit sin, God wants you to come to Him immediately. Like the prodigal son's father, God will run to meet you. He's waiting with open arms, knowing that the longer it takes you to come to Him, the greater opportunity the devil has to keep you away, thinking that you're unclean.

I want to assure you that God is not angry with you when you sin. Is He pleased when you sin? No, but we must continue to understand that God sees you through what Jesus did on the cross and who you are now in the spirit; and according to the Bible, He sees you as righteous and holy as long as you continue to trust in His righteousness alone as it is written, *Yet now he has reconciled in the body of his flesh through death, to present you holy and unblameable and unreproveable in his sight, if you continue in the faith grounded and settled, and be not moved away from the hope of the gospel...* [Colossians 1:21-23]

We know that Jesus, who is the exact image of God, never got angry with the tax collectors, prostitutes, adulterers, and other so-called "sinners" of His day. However, the only ones the Lord ever rebuked were those who were either operating in unbelief, or the self-righteous scribes and Pharisees who were counting on their own righteousness to make them right with God.

Furthermore, God does not accept or deal with us based on our

> I DO NOT FRUSTRATE THE GRACE OF GOD. FOR IF RIGHTEOUS-NESS COMES BY THE LAW, THEN CHRIST IS DEAD IN VAIN.
>
> *Galatians 2:21*

performance. If He did, then Jesus would have never come. Romans 5:8 says: *But God commended his love toward us, in that while we were yet sinners Christ died for us.* Tragically, while many Christians understand the truth of this verse, they fail to understand the great extent of God's grace—even after we are born again. The mindset is that while we are saved by grace, but once we are saved, we must perform satisfactorily in order for God to continue accepting us. This is not what the Bible teaches. Verses 9-10 of Romans 5 refers to the abundance of grace <u>after</u> being reconciled to God:

Much more then, being now justified by his blood, we shall be saved from wrath through him. For if, when we were enemies, we were reconciled to God by the death of his Son, much more, being reconciled, we shall be saved by his life.

FOR WE ARE THE CIRCUMCISION, WHICH WORSHIP GOD IN THE SPIRIT, AND REJOICE IN CHRIST JESUS, AND HAVE NO CONFIDENCE IN THE FLESH.

Philippians 3:3

Why Live Holy?

What shall we say then? Shall we continue in sin, that grace may abound?
ROMANS 6:1

FOR THE GRACE OF GOD THAT BRINGS SALVATION HAS APPEARED TO ALL MEN, TEACHING US THAT, DENYING UNGODLINESS AND WORLDLY LUSTS, WE SHOULD LIVE SOBERLY, RIGHTEOUSLY, AND GODLY IN THIS PRESENT WORLD.

Titus 2:11-12

One of the most common questions that arises when the true gospel is preached is "If God is not holding sin against us, then why should we live a holy life?" The apostle Paul faced this very same issue during his ministry, about which he wrote in chapter 6 of his letter to the Romans. Apparently, it had been reported throughout the region that Paul was preaching a message that encouraged sinful behavior so that good may come (Romans 3:8). Because of the fact that the true gospel is so almost unbelievably too good to be true news, when it is preached, this is the conclusion most people draw when they hear it—and for good reason.

The reason being is that we have grown up knowing only the bondage of a performance-based life. As children we were taught by our parents that if we misbehave we get punished, and if we behave we are rewarded. Guilt and shame are placed upon us for poor performance, and praise and honor are given to us in positive behavior. If you recite your A-B-Cs, then you get a praiseful pat on the head, but if you wet the bed you get a spanking. This begins a cycle of performance that grows into our "formative" years where we are seeking acceptance from not only our parents, but our teachers and friends, placing further demands on the level of our performance in order to be "accepted". And although our parents say their love is unconditional, their actions speak a different message—the message saying, "I'm ashamed of you" among other things when we mess up; and "I'm proud of you" only when we do something worthy of this praise. It's not their fault though. Our parents had parents just like them; and their parents had parents too.

It doesn't end there, however. As we grow into young adults, all the years of competitive sports, beauty pageants, class elections, and striving to be the best student, getting the best grades, and getting into the best college, turns us into what I call "performance-aholics". We want to be a part of the best fraternity, have the best looking girlfriend, throw the best parties, have the coolest car and clothes, all in combination with striving to excel in such a way that we can get the most prestigious and high-paying job after graduation. Then after entering the workforce, we are slung deeper into the performance pit where our salaries and promotions are based on our performance, and how we compare to our peers. Our friends and love relationships are only to the extent of how we make each other feel;

BUT NOW WE ARE DELIVERED FROM THE LAW, THAT BEING DEAD WHEREIN WE WERE HELD; THAT WE SHOULD SERVE IN NEWNESS OF SPIRIT, AND NOT IN THE OLDNESS OF THE LETTER.

Romans 7:6

I AM WHAT I AM

and as soon as someone is wronged, the friendship no longer exists. Love is something we "fall in" instead of it being a choice. Our romantic relationships are based mostly on emotion and physical attraction instead of commitment and the biblical truth that teaches us that we can be taught how to love one another (Titus 2:4). We submit to what we see on television and in the movies, and in the lives of people we exalt to such a high degree as being how life really is. We devote our lives to living in competition at work, then we involve ourselves in competitive sports or efforts to keep up with the Joneses to further boost our fragile little egos, so that we can, when before we wanted to impress our parents, now we are out to impress a potential mate, and perhaps win a little influence among friends and colleagues.

AND BE FOUND IN HIM, NOT HAVING MY OWN RIGHTEOUS- NESS, WHICH IS OF THE LAW, BUT THAT WHICH IS THROUGH THE FAITH OF CHRIST, THE RIGHTEOUS- NESS WHICH IS OF GOD BY FAITH.

Philippians 3:9

And this is only one end of the spectrum of performance. The other side involves a constant barrage of negativism the keeps a person under constant condemnation and under the control of life's circumstances. The old saying, "You are a product of your environment" gives rise to the notion that you are not worthy to receive any more than what you see. Instead of striving to excel to greater heights, these folks are kept in such a state that they cannot even look up. They hear words like, "You'll never measure up. You'll always be poor and live in the ghetto" never truly knowing anything else.

Typically both ends of the spectrum are exposed to a knowledge of God and religion in some way, but for the most part, this exposure only scratches the surface of the gospel message, teaching a watered-down, and mostly legalistic version of Christianity that relates perfectly with our performance mentality in order to please God.

The way most of us have grown up, it is no wonder why this conclusion was drawn when Paul preached the gospel, and still is when the true gospel is preached. How hard must it be to strip the years of conditioning from our minds and accept that we no longer have to perform in order to please the only One who matters—especially when we have been wrongfully taught that God also deals with us proportionate to our performance.

Nevertheless, the gospel is what it is, which is the power of God that leads to salvation. In its utmost simplicity, the true gospel strips away all of our own sense of self-worth, and self-degradation, putting all of us, Jew or Gentile, Catholic or Protestant, rich or poor, educated or uneducated, white or non-white, slave or free, neurosurgeon or janitor, moral or immoral, at the same level, leaving us only to trust in what Jesus did on the cross to make us right with God.

While the world teaches self-esteem, the gospel teaches Christ-esteem. Religion teaches what you must do to earn God's acceptance, but the gospel points to what Jesus did to make us not just accepted in the beloved, but highly favored. It does not matter what you have done or are doing, whether good or bad, but what matters is that you have come to the end of yourself and realized you have no power at all to be right with God, and that through faith in the righteous-

I AM WHAT I AM

ness of Jesus that is imparted to all who believe, you are righteous in the eyes of God.

Religion teaches that you must do A, B, and C to become worthy of salvation. But the gospel teaches that God only justifies the ungodly (Romans 4:5). Religion teaches that holiness is a route to salvation, but the gospel teaches that holiness is a fruit of salvation.

If this is the message you have heard before, then you have heard the true gospel and perhaps you have drawn the same conclusion as those in Paul's day. If the question, "If we are under God's grace by faith, then why should we live a holy life?" hasn't ever been asked by you (whether inwardly or outwardly), then perhaps you haven't heard the true gospel. Furthermore, for those who have shared the gospel with anyone and this question hasn't been raised, then maybe you should reconsider what gospel you are sharing.

Other than witnessing the power of God confirming the true gospel message, this conclusion is a telltale sign that you are preaching the same gospel that the Lord Jesus and Paul preached. Paul had asked two rhetorical questions in verses 1 and 15. The first question arose from what Paul had taught in chapter 5 concerning the abundant grace in comparison to sin. *What shall we say then? Shall we continue in sin, that grace may abound?* Paul's answer?

AND I, BRETHREN, IF I YET PREACH CIRCUMCISION, WHY DO I YET SUFFER PERSECUTION? THEN IS THE OFFENSE OF THE CROSS CEASED.

Galatians 5:11

You Have a New Nature

God forbid. How shall we, that are dead to sin, live any longer therein? Do you not know that so many of us as were baptized into Jesus Christ

49

were baptized into his death? Therefore we are buried with him by baptism into death. That like as Christ was raised up from the dead by the glory of the Father, even so we also should walk in the newness of life. For if we have been planted together in the likeness of his death, we shall be also in the likeness of his resurrection. [Romans 6:2-5]

Plain and simple, Paul's answer is, "Because you have a new nature; you don't have to live in sin anymore." Before you were born again, you were under the control of your sinful nature—the nature of the devil—that compelled you to lie, cheat, steal, curse, envy, lust, hate, and judge others. Your old nature was crucified with Christ, and now, being dead to sin, your new nature gives you the desire to live holy before God and man.

In my opinion, this is perhaps the most important teaching of the New Testament. Once we understand who we are in Christ, having a new godly nature, we can begin the journey of the victorious life Jesus died to give us. Then we can confidently quote this verse from Romans 8:37: *We are more than conquerors through him that loved us.*

The letters of Paul, Peter, James, and John express their frustration with the sinful behavior of believers, not fully understanding that they were no longer compelled to do such things, and that their sinful actions actually opened the door to the devil to come in and destroy. I think James said it well, *My brothers, these things ought not to be so.* [James 3:10] Why? Because they have a new nature—one that lives for God and not for sin. Consequently, this entire book's

AND SUCH WERE SOME OF YOU. BUT YOU ARE WASHED, BUT YOU ARE SANCTIFIED, BUT YOU ARE JUSTIFIED IN THE NAME OF THE LORD JESUS, AND BY THE SPIRIT OF OUR GOD.

1 Cor. 6:11

I AM WHAT I AM

purpose is to firmly establish the truth of who we are in Christ.

The Bible says, *He that is dead is freed from sin.* [Romans 6:7] In this context the word freed means that you have been set free from the power and control of sin through the death of the Lord Jesus. Being set free doesn't necessarily mean that you are free however.

Let me give you an example of how someone can be freed, but not be free. In 1862, President Abraham Lincoln signed the Emancipation Proclamation, which gave freedom to all the slaves in the United States. Legally from that moment on, every slave had been set free, but not all slaves were actually free. Why? This occurred for several reasons. Firstly, because word had not yet reached all the slaves and slaveholders that they had been set free. Secondly, while word had been received of the emancipation, many either did not believe it, or refused to obey it. Consequently, if a slave was happy being a slave, although he had been set free, he could still have remained a slave.

The same is true of us in Christ. Jesus said, *If you continue in my word, then are you my disciples indeed; and you shall know the truth, and the truth shall make you free.* [John 8:31-32] Not until you receive knowledge or word of the truth and act upon it (faith) will you be truly free. Just as the fact that God, through Jesus, has provided salvation for all mankind, but not all men (or women) will be saved. Religion has taught for so long that although you have been set free from sin, you still have this old sinful nature lurking and lingering around, forcing you into sinful behavior. That's simply not what

AND I WILL PUT MY SPIRIT WITHIN YOU, AND CAUSE YOU TO WALK IN MY STATUTES, AND YOU SHALL KEEP MY JUDGMENTS, AND DO THEM.

Ezekiel 36:27

Scripture teaches although we have Bible translations that do. Unfortunately, the devil has translated some of the versions of the Bible, which have proven to blind the eyes and minds of the truth.

According to some translations, you are just a prisoner out on parole, still under the control of your old warden who can bring you back to prison at any time. This is the truth and I pray that you will receive it. You <u>were</u> a prisoner and slave to your sinful nature, but Jesus has unlocked the cell door to freedom and we must, through faith, push open the door to freedom. Once we receive the gospel, our sinful nature dies, and God imparts His nature into our new spirit (new wine into new bottles), making us new creatures in Christ. Therefore, you are not forced to submit to the temptation to sin and consequently, you have no excuses like "I just couldn't help myself" when you blow it.

Now some of you may be asking, "Why then, after being born again, do I sin, if I now no longer have a sinful nature?" When you are born again, your spirit is changed—not your mind. Your mind is like a computer, which will operate according to its programming. Your mind was programmed by your "old man" (sinful nature) and consequently, it needs re-programming. Romans 12:2 says, *Be not conformed to this world, but be transformed by the renewing of your mind, that you may prove what is that good and acceptable, and perfect will of God.* A lifetime of sin has left a residue of sinful behavior that can change through a commitment to renewing your mind through God's word.

I AM WHAT I AM

A great illustration of this truth occurs when a person's physical body dies. For a period of time, although being dead, the body can appear to be alive. Having been in law enforcement, I saw many dead bodies, and some of those dead bodies moved and even uttered sounds. I heard the story about a man who worked in a hospital morgue, and late one night he was processing a dead body when all of sudden the body just sat up with its eyes open. Needless to say, the worker was wrought with fear, and went to get help.

He summoned a doctor, and after examining the body, the doctor pushed it back down on the table. The man was still dead, but sometimes the body can bear signs of life when in reality they are dead. This same thing is true with our old sinful nature—it is really dead, but it can display signs of being alive.

Although signs or appearance of life in a dead body are generally short-lived due to decay, the manifestations of the old nature seem to linger longer than they should in comparison. The reason for this is because most Christians have been taught that their old sinful nature has not died, but still exists and thrives. If a person believes this deception, then it makes sense that the effects of the old sinful nature would continue as long as they continued to believe it.

The main character in the movie *Psycho* illustrates this point accurately. Although his mother had died years before, the son kept her body dressed and sitting in a chair, believing she was still alive to encourage him to kill people. You can keep the manifestation of your old nature alive if you continue to believe it is alive, and this is why

LIKEWISE RECKON ALSO YOURSELVES TO BE DEAD INDEED UNTO SIN, BUT ALIVE UNTO GOD THROUGH JESUS CHRIST OUR LORD.

Romans 6:11

it is so very important for you to know that the old sinful nature is dead.

The title *Psycho* fits perfectly with the behavior of the main character—not the killing, but the way he was thinking. The difference between a sane person and an insane person is the way they think. The character in *Psycho* had been deceived in his mind that his mother was telling him to do these terrible acts. Similarly, when you believe the old sinful nature is still alive, you can be deceived into doing things you shouldn't (Galatians 5:17). Psychotic behavior is changed not by focusing on the behavior, but on changing the way a person thinks. This is why the Scripture teaches that you are *transformed by the renewing of your mind, that you may prove what is that good, and acceptable, and perfect will of God.* [Romans 12:2]

The two most important verses in Romans 6 convey what Paul truly wants every believer to know. Through this revelation, we can destroy any teaching that suggests that a Christian is still under the power and control of sin. Moreover, these passages are absolutely vital to walking in the newness of life and the likeness of His resurrection (Romans 6:4-5). *Knowing this, that our old man is crucified with him, that the body of sin might be destroyed, that henceforth we should not serve sin. Knowing that Christ being raised from the dead dies no more; death has no more dominion over him. For in that he died, he died unto sin once; but in that he lives, he lives unto God. Likewise reckon* (or conclude also in yourself) *yourselves to be dead indeed unto sin, but alive unto God through Jesus Christ our Lord.* [Romans 6:6, 9-11]

THIS I SAY THEN, WALK IN THE SPIRIT, AND YOU SHALL NOT FULFILL THE LUST OF THE FLESH.

Galatians 5:16

I AM WHAT I AM

Verses 6-11 support the apostle Paul's conclusion he made in verses 4-5 that we should be walking in the newness of life and the likeness of His resurrection. However, he stresses that in order to walk in the likeness of His resurrection, we must first know (and accept by faith) that our old man has been crucified with Him, and we are dead to sin, being freed by the death and resurrection of the Lord Jesus. Furthermore, because Jesus died to sin once, we should conclude that we must die to sin only once as well.

I simply cannot stress this enough because these passages illustrate the theme of this book—knowing and submitting to who you are in Christ. The Bible is teaching that it is impossible for a Christian to walk in the newness of life and the likeness of His resurrection without first laying the foundation of your old sinful nature being crucified and dead. This truth is a daily meditation for me, as it should be for all Christians. Because when temptation comes, the Spirit can bring this one truth back to your remembrance, knowing that since you are dead to the old sinful nature, you do not have to obey, but, as the Scripture teaches, *yield yourselves unto God, as those that are alive from the dead, and your members as instruments of righteousness unto God.* [Romans 6:13]

Many Christian churches teach that you must die to sin daily, but this is not what Scripture teaches. Again, I point to Romans 6 that says that you must conclude that as Jesus died to sin once, you must consider yourself dead without a doubt to sin once and for all. This is what the word "Likewise" means—in other words, "in the

> FOR THEY BEING IGNORANT OF GOD'S RIGHTEOUSNESS, AND GOING ABOUT TO ESTABLISH THEIR OWN RIGHTEOUSNESS, HAVE NOT SUBMITTED THEMSELVES UNTO THE RIGHTEOUSNESS OF GOD.
>
> *Romans 10:3*

same way." Paul wrote in 1 Corinthians 15:30, *I die daily*, and many teachers of the Bible have inferred that he means that Paul died to his sinful nature on a daily basis. Again, this violates what Paul taught in Romans 6, and actually refers to the sufferings he was facing on a daily basis, which oftentimes led to near death. Paul is actually justifying his sufferings, proving that he was fully persuaded that the word of God was true in that he would rise again in the resurrection.

WHERE-
FORE, MY
BRETHREN,
YOU ALSO
ARE
BECOME
DEAD TO
THE LAW
BY THE
BODY OF
CHRIST.

Romans 7:4

Most importantly, however, the phrase *I die daily* can be related to our walk in Christ and carrying the cross. We must die to ourselves on a daily basis so that the character of Christ can be revealed in our lives. This is what humility is, my friends—to trust completely in what Jesus did on the cross to make us right with God; trust in what the word of God teaches, and then apply it to your daily life.

Therefore, you must live according to the fact that you died (were crucified with Christ) to sin once, and were risen in the newness of life (having the nature of Christ living in and through you). The apostle Paul wrote, *I am crucified* (past tense) *with Christ; nevertheless I live. Yet not I but Christ lives* (present tense) *in me; and the life which I now live in the flesh, I live by the faith of the Son of God, who loved me, and gave himself for me.* [Galatians 2:20]

The typical Christian, after being born again, makes a commitment to pursuing holiness. However, most often it is done through his or her own strength, which amounts to living under the law. Holiness is a fruit or byproduct of your relationship with the Lord and cannot be achieved in your own strength. In fact, the moment you begin trying to live according to the law, you will find yourself under the dominion and control of sin. *For sin shall not have dominion over you. For you are not under the law, but under grace.* [Romans 6:14] *Christ has become of no effect unto you, whosoever of you are justified by the law; you are fallen from grace.* [Galatians 5:4]

Embracing the truth of the new creature will help keep you living according to grace—and not of works. The Bible says, *For in Christ Jesus neither circumcision avails anything, nor uncircumcision, but a new creature. And as many as walk according to this rule, peace be on them, and mercy, and upon the Israel of God.* [Galatians 6:15-16]

In Romans 7, Paul addresses them who are trying to live according to the law. *Do you not know, brethren, (for I speak to them that know the law,) how that the law has dominion over a man as long as he lives?* After illustrating the bondage to sin by comparing it to marriage, Paul begins to describe the effects of living by the law through what occurs before we are born again, and then the struggle that ensues once a person attempts to live by the law. I discuss this issue in greater detail in the chapter entitled "Spirit vs. Flesh."

After relating the frustration involved in legalism, Paul concludes his point by saying, *I delight in the law of God after the inward man. But I see another law in my members, warring against the law of my mind, and bringing me into captivity to the law of sin, which is in my members. O wretched man that I am! Who shall deliver me from the body of this death? I thank God through Jesus Christ our Lord. So then with the mind I myself serve the law of God; but with the flesh the law of*

> FOR SIN SHALL NOT HAVE DOMINION OVER YOU. FOR YOU ARE NOT UNDER THE LAW, BUT UNDER GRACE.
>
> *Romans 6:14*

sin. [Romans 7:22-25]

What many people do not realize is that sin actually derives its power from the law. The Bible is so very clear concerning this truth, but many of us have been blinded by it. The Bible says, *the strength of sin is the law.* [1 Corinthians 15:56] The apostle Paul wrote in Romans 7:9: *For I was alive without the law once, but when the commandment came, sin revived, and I died.* What Paul is saying is that when he was a child, he did not understand that disobedience was not only against his parents, but against the commandments of God. Sin, although present, was not imputed or counted against him, and the sinful nature existed, but had no power to condemn because as the Scripture teaches, *For until the law sin was in the world; but sin is not imputed when there is no law.* [Romans 5:13] Therefore, the sinful nature was in essence lying dormant, waiting for the power of the law to come and kill. But when he understood with his heart that he had offended God (the commandment), the sinful nature came back to life, and by the law, it killed him.

Many people have been taught that we became sinners after we first committed sin (and understood it by the commandment) and that sin did not dwell in us until we submitted to it. This is false and contrary to what the Bible teaches in Romans. We were all born into sin because of the sin of Adam (Romans 5:12), but according to Scripture, sin is not counted against us when we do not understand the law (Romans 5:13). Therefore, we can truly embrace the fact that since we did nothing to make ourselves sinners, and consequently,

WHERE-
FORE THE
LAW WAS
OUR
SCHOOL-
MASTER
TO BRING
US UNTO
CHRIST,
THAT WE
MIGHT BE
JUSTIFIED
BY FAITH.

Galatians 3:24

I AM WHAT I AM

we can do nothing to make ourselves righteous, other than submit ourselves to the righteousness of Jesus, we, being made righteous by faith, can do nothing to make ourselves sinners again, short of rejecting the righteousness of Jesus, hoping that our own righteousness will be enough. Paul wrote a powerful truth to anyone who is trying to impress God by his or her own good works or holiness: *I do not frustrate the grace of God. For if righteousness comes by the law, then Christ is dead in vain.* [Galatians 2:21]

If you think you are righteous by what you have done or are doing, then you are telling God that the suffering of His precious Son was for nothing. It is either all Jesus or all you, my brothers and sisters. It is either all grace or all works—not a little bit of each. Grace doesn't make up the difference; it is all you need. The Bible says: *And if by grace, then it is no more of works; otherwise grace is no more grace. But if it be of works, then it is no more grace; otherwise work is no more work.* [Romans 11:6]

Keep the Devil at Bay

Be sober, be vigilant, because your adversary the devil, as a roaring lion, walks about, seeking whom he may devour, whom resist steadfast in the faith, knowing that the same afflictions are accomplished in your brethren that are in the world. [1 Peter 5:8-9]

In addition to understanding that in Christ we are now dead to sin, having a new nature, the Bible teaches that we should also live holy in order to hinder the devil's destructive work in our lives. How-

SUBMIT YOURSELVES THEREFORE UNTO GOD. RESIST THE DEVIL AND HE WILL FLEE FROM YOU.

James 4:7

ever, it is only because of our understanding and belief in the truth of our old sinful nature having been crucified with Him (Romans 6:6) will we ever be able to fully resist the devil's temptations and deceptions. This means that Paul's answer to the second question posed in Romans 6:15 (*What then? Shall we sin because we are not under the law, but under grace?*) is dependent entirely upon our revelation of being dead to sin once and walking according to the likeness of His resurrection or the new creature.

Most Christians have understood the importance of holiness in the context of keeping the devil from getting a foothold in a person's life. However, many have been attempting to resist the devil without having first understood what the apostle Paul wanted them to know first, which was that their old man was crucified with him—so much that he stated the truth about being dead to sin <u>eight times</u> in Romans 6:1-11.

Paul's response to the question in Romans 6:15 simply repeats what he taught concerning to whom we should yield ourselves—whether *as instruments of unrighteousness unto sin* or *instruments of righteousness unto God*, of which he ties to recognizing that you are alive from the dead (Romans 6:13).

Do you not know that to whom you yield yourselves servants to obey, his servants you are to whom you obey, whether of sin unto death, or of obedience unto righteousness? [Romans 6:16]

This passage is the foundational spiritual law by which Satan was legally able to hold the human race in bondage because of Adam's

ALWAYS BEARING ABOUT IN THE BODY THE DYING OF THE LORD JESUS, THAT THE LIFE ALSO OF JESUS MIGHT BE MADE MANIFEST IN OUR BODY.

2 Cor. 4:10

transgression. When Adam and Eve submitted to the deception of the serpent, transgressing the command of God, they legally transferred all the dominion and authority God had given them on earth to the devil.

In relation to our standing in Christ, the Bible teaches that the Lord Jesus has freed us from the bondage of sin by His death, and while we should now consider ourselves to be servants to God in Christ, we can still yield to the devil's temptations, which continue to bring about death.

God, through Jesus, has already dealt with sin at the cross, and when you are born again, sin no longer separates you from having relationship with God. However, yielding to the devil can hinder, disrupt, and damage your fellowship with God and with other people. There are many Christians who believe that God can only deal with you when you are walking in total purity—without any sin in your life. This is simply not what the Scripture teaches about God's grace—that it is not dependent upon our performance. Otherwise, God could not deal with anyone because we all fail to live up to the standard of the Lord Jesus in our flesh.

The reason God wants us to maintain a holy lifestyle is because He loves us and wants only the best for His children. By yielding ourselves to temptation, we are giving a place for the devil to come in and to steal, kill, and destroy. Yielding to sin can make your heart hardened toward God whereby you cannot hear His voice and be directed by the Spirit. Yielding to sin can hinder the Lord's blessings

TO WIT, THAT GOD WAS IN CHRIST, RECONCIL-ING THE WORLD UNTO HIMSELF, NOT IMPUTING THEIR TRES-PASSES UNTO THEM; AND HAS COMMIT-TED UNTO US THE WORD OF RECON-CILIATION.

2 Cor. 5:19

and calling on your life. Yielding to sin can damage relationships with people. Yielding to sin can bring about sickness, and other forces that destroy your body. And finally, yielding to sin can damage your ability to minister to others because of condemnation, or because like it or not, people still look at the outward appearance.

Paul teaches about the fruit that can be produced by the Christian when he or she yields to sin as compared to when he or she yields to God. Because it appeared that the Roman Christians were still yielding themselves to sin, Paul was forced to correct them by writing, *I speak after the manner of men because of the infirmity of your flesh. For as you have yielded your members servants to uncleanness and to iniquity unto iniquity; even so now yield your members servants to righteousness unto holiness.* [Romans 6:19]

As I mentioned before, holiness is a byproduct of our relationship or right standing with God. Therefore, when we embrace the fact that we are the righteousness of God by faith in Jesus Christ (2 Corinthians 5:21), we shall bring forth fruit of holiness (John 15:5).

And this is what the Bible is teaching in these passages. Paul makes the comparison to the fruit produced in sin, and the fruit that should be produced in the Christian who understands the fact that he is dead to sin and alive unto God as it is written, *For when you were the servants of sin, you were free from righteousness. What fruit did you have then in those things whereof you are now ashamed? For the end of those things is death. But now being made free from sin, and become servants to God, you have your fruit unto holiness, and the end*

FOR WE ARE HIS WORKMANSHIP, CREATED IN CHRIST JESUS UNTO GOOD WORKS, WHICH GOD HAD BEFORE ORDAINED THAT WE SHOULD WALK IN THEM.

Ephesians 2:10

everlasting life. For the wages of sin is death; but the gift of God is eternal life through Jesus Christ our Lord. [Romans 6:20-23]

Once again, Paul, referring specifically to what he wrote in verse 6, repeats the truth about being dead to sin and being made free from it, saying that the Christian should be bearing fruit in the form of holiness. The final comparison (v. 23) is perhaps the most provocative and simplistic and at the same time, represents what Paul was teaching in Romans 5, which is the stark difference between sin and death by the law, and eternal life by grace through Jesus Christ.

Many Christians have gotten so caught up in the wordiness of Paul's dictation that they fail to comprehend the basic theme of this teaching—that the grace of God has broken the power of sin brought on by the law, and that by understanding that as Christ died to sin, we too, when we were born again, died to sin, and should now walk in the newness of life and the likeness of His resurrection.

This is Paul's answer to these compelling questions. As the butterfly and eagle fly, a Christian should live a holy life. Why? Because it is his nature to do so.

FOR THE LAW OF THE SPIRIT OF LIFE IN CHRIST JESUS HAS MADE ME FREE FROM THE LAW OF SIN AND DEATH.

Romans 8:2

6
You Are Spirit

Jesus answered, Verily, verily I say unto you, Except a man be born of water and of the Spirit, he cannot enter into the kingdom of God. That which is born of the flesh is flesh; and that which is born of the Spirit is spirit.

JOHN 3:5-6

Of all verses of scripture that are misunderstood, I believe this verse from John 3 ranks at or near the top. From what I have heard from others, many Christians interpret this verse to support the absolute necessity of water baptism as a means of salvation. Hence they conclude that water baptism is being born of water and being born of the Spirit is receiving the Holy Spirit as the Lord Jesus did when He was baptized and then coming out of the water, He received the Holy Spirit (Matthew 3:16).

As God is three-dimensional (Father, Son, Holy Spirit), we are three-dimensional as well, existing as spirit, soul, and body.

As logical as it sounds, it simply is a misinterpretation of scripture. My intention with this book is not to teach about the necessity of water baptism as a part of God's will for all believers. However, the Bible teaches that baptism in water is simply an outward symbol or confession of our own death, burial, and resurrection in the newness of life (Romans 6:4; 1 Peter 3:21).

Moreover, the Bible uses the word baptism to refer to a number of things—most importantly the baptism or immersion into Christ (Romans 6:3; Acts 2:38). When Peter answered the multitude in Jerusalem, *Repent and be baptized in the name of Jesus Christ for the remission of sins, and you shall receive the gift of the Holy Ghost*, he was not ordering everyone to be dunked in water using the name of Jesus. Rather, and this bears out in the totality of scripture, he was telling the people to turn back to God through repentance (or a change of attitude toward their right standing with God) and be immersed or baptized into the body of Christ by grace through faith (Ephesians 2:8), and your sins will be washed away—not with water—but with the blood of Jesus. In fact, Peter makes the same exhortation in Acts 3:19 when he says, *Repent therefore, and be converted, that your sins may be blotted out...*, indicating that the baptism he refers to is actually the new birth—the immersion into Christ and not the ceremonial expression we know today as baptism.

Finally, the Bible teaches that there are many baptisms (water, Spirit) but only one baptism that brings salvation—that is the baptism into the body of Christ (Ephesians 4:5).

In John 3:5-8 the Lord is trying to teach about the clear distinction between the natural birth and the spiritual birth. Why people misunderstand this verse is compelling to me because the Lord clarified what He said at the end of the verse: *That which is born of the*

FOR MAN LOOKS ON THE OUTWARD APPEAR-ANCE, BUT THE LORD LOOKS ON THE HEART.

1 Samuel 16:7

flesh (of water) *is flesh; and that which is born of the Spirit is spirit.*

However, much like Nicodemus, many Christians have failed to understand even the most foundational of spiritual truths. From our natural birth, we are born into sin, and take upon the nature or spirit of the devil (Psalm 51:5; Ephesians 2:3). The sin of Adam and the death it produced was passed down to all men, which is why the Scripture has concluded that all have sinned (Romans 5:12). This sinful nature inherited from Adam is what drove us to commit the actions of sin (Romans 7:5).

Therefore, your actions that amounted to sins did not make you a sinner. Rather, the sinful nature you were born with drove you to sin. In simple terms, you sinned because you were born a sinner. Consequently, your sinful actions did not make you a sinner any more than your good works made you righteous. I stress these points—not to condemn you, but for you to understand the necessity of being born again and what occurred at this new birth.

So, we conclude that if you were initially born a sinner, then when you were born again, you were born again righteous, holy, and pure (Ephesians 4:24).

Until this sinful nature is crucified, it is impossible to have the intimate relationship that God desires. Jesus said, *God is a Spirit. And they that worship him must worship him in spirit and in truth.* [John 4:24] If your spirit is, by nature, the spirit of disobedience, any direct contact with God will kill you. This is why Jesus said that new wine cannot be poured into old bottles, *else the new wine will burst the*

TO THE GENERAL ASSEMBLY AND CHURCH OF THE FIRST-BORN, WHICH ARE WRITTEN IN HEAVEN, AND TO GOD THE JUDGE OF ALL, AND TO THE SPIRITS OF JUST MEN MADE PERFECT.

Hebrews 12:23

bottles, and be spilled, and the bottles shall perish. [Luke 5:37]

Since God is a Spirit, your salvation is done in your spirit. As we learn from the Bible that the spirit realm, the things of the spirit, or the things unseen always have dominance over natural, fleshy, or earthy things. God created the world in the spirit realm (using His word, which is spirit) before it became a natural reality (Hebrews 11:3).

In order to truly comprehend these truths, you must stop looking for your salvation in your flesh. The Bible says: *Now this I say, brethren, that flesh and blood cannot inherit the kingdom of God; neither does corruption inherit incorruption.* [1 Corinthians 15:50]

What the majority of Christians fail to comprehend is that their salvation was done in their spirit—not in their flesh or mind. The work of the Holy Spirit upon receiving the gift of eternal life is to give life to our new spirit. Therefore, our old spirit is crucified and dead to our past sinful lives (Galatians 2:20).

If you are born again, your spirit is divine, perfect, and is the same spirit as Christ. Many Christians choke on this truth and this is the reason they are not walking in the victory the Lord died to give them. I'm not saying that you are God, or that you are equal to God. But I am saying that you are a partaker of the divine nature (2 Peter 1:4); and you have received a portion of God's fullness by grace through faith (John 1:16). Being a partaker means that you have been given a portion of God, which is His Spirit indwelling in you. In fact, you are 1/3 divine.

AND OF HIS FULLNESS HAVE ALL WE RECEIVED, AND GRACE FOR GRACE. FOR THE LAW WAS GIVEN BY MOSES, BUT GRACE AND TRUTH CAME BY JESUS CHRIST.

John 1:16-17

The Bible says: *Do you not know that your bodies are the members of Christ? Shall I then take the members of Christ, and make them members of a harlot? God forbid. What? Do you not know that he which is joined to a harlot is one body? For two, he said, shall be one flesh. <u>But he that is joined unto the Lord is one spirit.</u>* [1 Corinthians 6:15-17]

The Bible also says that your spirit is perfect—the same spirit as Christ. *But you are not in the flesh, but in the Spirit, if so be that the Spirit of God dwell in you. Now if any man have not the Spirit of Christ, he is none of his.* [Romans 8:9]

For by one offering he has perfected forever them that are sanctified. [Hebrews 10:14]

The Bible clearly supports this truth: *Herein is our love made perfect, that we may have boldness in the day of judgment; because as he is, so are we in this world.* [1 John 4:17] I like to say it this way, "As Jesus said, 'He who has seen Me has seen the Father,' we should desire to confidently say, 'He who has seen me has seen Jesus.'"

However, after reading this, most people immediately look in the mirror (at their flesh) and conclude that this statement would be a lie. Their flesh is weak and for the most part their minds are focused on fear, death, and worry. As I explained before, you cannot look at your body and soul to see Christ in you, because He is found in your spirit. The Bible says: *Wherefore henceforth we know no man after the flesh. Yea though we have known Christ after the flesh, yet now henceforth we know him no more. Therefore, if any man is in Christ, he is a new creature. Old things are passed away; behold, all things are*

FOR THEY THAT ARE AFTER THE FLESH DO MIND THE THINGS OF THE FLESH; BUT THEY THAT ARE AFTER THE SPIRIT THE THINGS OF THE SPIRIT.

Romans 8:5

I AM WHAT I AM

become new. And all things are of God, who has reconciled us to himself by Jesus Christ, and has given to us the ministry of reconciliation. [2 Corinthians 5:16-18]

Teaching the same principle to the Philippians, Paul wrote, *For we are the circumcision, which worship God in the spirit, and rejoice in Christ Jesus, and have no confidence in the flesh.* [Philippians 3:3] Additionally, in his letter to the Romans: *For he is not a Jew, which is one outwardly; neither is that circumcision, which is outward in the flesh. But he is a Jew, which is one inwardly; and circumcision is that of the heart, in the spirit, and not in the letter, whose praise is not of men, but of God.* [Romans 2:28-29]

Paul also wrote, *For God is my witness, whom I serve with my spirit in the gospel of his Son...* [Romans 1:9] This clearly teaches that our service to God is done with your new godly spirit, and you must serve Him according to grace—not according to your own obedience to the law.

An understanding of the truth that your salvation was done in your spirit will most certainly answer many questions most of you have asked since you were born again. God is a spirit, and He only sees you through your spirit and through the sacrifice of Jesus.

Now your journey is to become completely transformed into the image of God by allowing the character of Christ to be magnified in your body (Philippians 1:20) through the renewing of your mind (Romans 12:2) which is accomplished through thoughtful study of God's word. Any good works, obedience and faithfulness

BUT THE NATURAL MAN RECEIVES NOT THE THINGS OF THE SPIRIT OF GOD. FOR THEY ARE FOOLISHNESS UNTO HIM. NEITHER CAN HE KNOW THEM, BECAUSE THEY ARE SPIRITUALLY DISCERNED.

1 Cor. 2:14

will simply be a byproduct of your relationship with the Lord.

The illustration I gave before of the new Christian and his frustration with understanding the reality of the new creature is pervasive throughout the body of Christ. You were told that your life would change, but you haven't realized any fruit in this change. The reason being is that you are only looking at your flesh and thinking with your mind instead of looking into the spirit and thinking with your heart. Change has been presented as something accomplished by you instead of simply through the process of planting the word of God in your heart and bearing fruit as a result.

Once you discover the truth that your salvation is complete in your spirit (Colossians 2:10) the rest of your life is a journey toward apprehending the mark of the high calling of God in Christ Jesus. You will never fully arrive—meaning in complete body and soul— until you receive your glorified body and completely renewed mind (1 Corinthians 15:49-54; 1 Corinthians 13:12). But, as the Scripture says, *Beloved now we are the sons of God, and it does not yet appear what we shall be; but we know that, when he shall appear, we shall be like him; for we shall see him as he is. And every man that has this hope in him purifies himself, even as he is pure.* [1 John 3:2-3]

I take this passage to mean that during the journey of our lives in Christ, (if we continue to seek Him with all our heart) we will see the Lord in a greater way (as He is), which will cause us to reflect His nature in our outward actions.

NOW HE WHICH ESTAB-LISHES US WITH YOU IN CHRIST, AND HAS ANOINTED US IS GOD, WHO HAS ALSO SEALED US, AND GIVEN THE EARNEST OF THE SPIRIT IN OUR HEARTS.

2 Cor. 1:21-22

Eternal Redemption

Neither by the blood of goats and calves, but by his own blood he entered in once into the holy place, having obtained eternal redemption for us.

HEBREWS 9:12

Knowing that Jesus is no longer on the cross and isn't suffering and dying for anyone currently, we can rightly conclude that the sacrifice of Jesus was done once and for all. Not only does this include *all* people, but *all* people for *all* time. The Bible confirms this truth in the following verses of scripture:

And he is the propitiation (atoning sacrifice or mercy seat) *for our sins; and not for ours only, but also for the sins of the whole world.* [1 John 2:2]

By the which will we are sanctified through the offering of the body of Jesus Christ <u>once for all</u>. And every priest stood daily ministering and offering oftentimes the same sacrifices, which can never take away sins. But this man, after he had <u>offered one sacrifice for sins forever</u>, sat down on the right hand of God. From henceforth expecting till his enemies be made his footstool. For by <u>one offering he has perfected forever them</u>

71

that are sanctified. [Hebrews 10:10-14]

Additionally, we can rightly conclude that since we are already forgiven of our sins forever, there is no need to ask or seek forgiveness for sins committed after we receive Christ. The Bible says, *As you have therefore received Christ Jesus the Lord, so walk in him.* [Colossians 2:6] We receive Christ by grace through faith and therefore, we should walk by faith in the truth that His sacrifice has completely absolved us from any guilt. The Bible also says: *And hereby we know that we are of the truth, and shall assure our hearts before him. For if our heart condemn us, God is greater than our heart, and knows all things. Beloved, if our heart condemn us not, then we have confidence toward God.* [1 John 3:19-21]

WHO IS HE THAT CONDEMNS? IT IS CHRIST THAT DIED, YEA RATHER, THAT IS RISEN AGAIN, WHO IS EVEN AT THE RIGHT HAND OF GOD, WHO ALSO MAKES INTERCESSION FOR US.

Romans 8:34

Notice that this verse does not say that God is the one who condemns us when we sin; rather it is our own heart or conscience that brings condemnation. Many Christians believe that the Holy Spirit brings conviction on a person, when the Bible teaches that it is our own conscience that brings conviction (John 8:9). God is not the condemner; He is the Savior (Romans 8:34).

This verse teaches us that because of what the Lord did on the cross and through His resurrection, we, as born again believers, can be assured in our hearts that God's grace is greater than any sinful act or failure on our part. This is the confidence that we have and must walk in.

Here's another passage from Isaiah 32, *And the work of righteousness shall be peace; and the effect of righteousness quietness and assur-*

ance for ever. [Isaiah 32:17]

Paul taught these same truths in his letter to the Romans. *Moreover the law entered, that the offense might abound. But where sin abounded, grace did much more abound. That as sin has reigned unto death, even so might grace reign through righteousness unto eternal life by Jesus Christ our Lord.* [Romans 5:20-21]

Some of you may be concluding that I am condoning sin, and that God doesn't care if you remain in sin. If you are, then I know that I'm teaching the same gospel that Paul taught because this same conclusion was drawn of him. I want to assure that in no way am I encouraging anyone to live in sin. What I am doing is placing our main focus on the extremely high value of the sacrifice of Jesus and the greatness of God's grace, instead of concentrating on sin, which, unfortunately, is what most churches are doing. By my exalting the cross and the grace of God, it appears that I am minimizing sin, but I'm not. Sin is bad; it destroys people and we should not ignore it. But God's grace and the suffering of the Lord Jesus are so much greater than any sin. In fact, chapter 6 of Romans addresses the very same point: *What shall we say then? Shall we continue in sin, that grace may abound?* [v. 1]

I'll give the same answer as Paul: *God forbid. How shall we, that are dead to sin, live any longer therein? Do you not know that so many of us as were baptized into Jesus Christ were baptized into his death? Therefore we are buried with him by baptism into death. That like as Christ was raised from the dead by the glory of the Father, even so we*

FOR BY ONE OFFERING HE HAS PERFECTED FOREVER THEM THAT ARE SANCTI- FIED.

Hebrews 10:14

also should walk in newness of life. [vv. 2-4]

Paul was simply telling the body of Christ that God's grace is greater than any sin we can commit—before and after receiving the gift of salvation. Furthermore, he said that once we are in Christ, we are no longer servants of sin, but servants of God. What provoked this question is our own misunderstanding of the magnitude of God's grace and the fact that our salvation was done in the spirit.

As Paul taught in Romans 5, that we were made sinners by the disobedience of Adam, our own personal sin, to a lesser degree, has nothing to do with our sinfulness. Rather, since we were born into sin, we can do nothing to make ourselves more sinful; and conversely, we cannot do anything to earn the grace of God. Either way, because of Adam's transgression, we need a Savior.

These verses declare that the grace of God has nothing to do with either our sinfulness or our own righteousness, but everything to do with what Jesus did for us.

Wherefore, as by one man sin entered into the world, and death by sin; and so death passed upon all men, <u>for that all have sinned.</u> (For until the law sin was in the world; but sin is not imputed when there is no law. Nevertheless death reigned from Adam to Moses, even over them that had not sinned after the similitude of Adam's transgression, who is the figure of him that was to come.

But not as the offense, so also is the free gift. For if through the offense of one many be dead, much more the grace of God, and the gift by grace, which is by one man Jesus Christ, has abounded unto many.

NOT BY WORKS OF RIGHTEOUSNESS WHICH WE HAVE DONE, BUT ACCORDING TO HIS MERCY HE SAVED US, BY THE WASHING OF REGENERATION, AND RENEWING OF THE HOLY GHOST.

Titus 3:5

I AM WHAT I AM

And not as it was by one that sinned, so is the gift. For the judgment was by one to condemnation, but the free gift is of many offenses unto justification.

For if by one man's offense death reigned by one; much more they which receive abundance of grace and of the gift of righteousness shall reign in life by one, Jesus Christ.)

Therefore as by the offense of one judgment came upon all men to condemnation; even so by the righteousness of one the free gift came upon all men unto justification of life.

For as by one man's disobedience many were made sinners, so by the obedience of one shall many be made righteous. [Romans 5:12-19]

One of the false teachings prevalent in the body of Christ is that if, as a Christian, you commit a sin, then you are no longer saved, and that unless you repent and become saved again, you will perish. As I said before, this mindset gives birth to a roller coaster ride filled with sinning, repenting, sinning, repenting, being saved, then lost, then saved, then lost, over and over again.

I've even heard of one teaching that says that you must confess every sin you commit before you can be "right" with God again. If this is true, how can a person like me, who was without Christ for over 30 years of my life, remember each and every sin I ever committed? Will God bring these things to my remembrance?

No, the blood of Jesus has wiped away all my sins—past, present, and future, and therefore, God does not remember them. *For I will be merciful to their unrighteousness, and their sins and their iniquities*

BUT IS NOW MADE MANIFEST BY THE APPEARING OF OUR SAVIOR JESUS CHRIST, WHO HAS ABOLISHED DEATH, AND HAS BROUGHT LIFE AND IMMORTAL-ITY TO LIGHT THROUGH THE GOSPEL.

2 Timothy 1:10

will I remember no more. [Hebrews 8:12]

Jesus said that if we came to Him, He would give us rest for our souls (Matthew 11:28-29). This attitude of being saved then lost and over and over each day doesn't compute to rest in my soul. The truth is that this rest the Lord spoke of is what the sabbath of the old testament foreshadowed. If you read Hebrews 3-4 you will learn that the true sabbath is being able to rest in Christ by faith.

The devil wants you to focus on sin because sin is of the flesh, but life is of the Sprit. To use a baseball term, if you are focused on your sin, you are throwing one right down the middle and the devil is going to hit it (and you) right out of the ballpark.

Has anyone ever told you that once you are born again, you cannot sin?

The Bible says that you have been sealed by the Holy Spirit until the day of redemption (Ephesians 4:30). This means that your spirit has been sealed or protected—in that it cannot be corrupted by a sin of the flesh. We sin and fall short in our bodies and minds every day, but in your spirit, you are righteous, pure, and holy—as holy as the Lord Jesus—and because of this seal, your spirit retains this condition regardless of what we do in our physical bodies.

The term being sealed means that something has been stamped (with a signet or private mark) for security or preservation, or sealed up or preserved. We can look at being sealed in three similar ways, all of which are effective in illustrating how your spirit has been sealed.

FOR HE THAT IS ENTERED INTO HIS REST, HE ALSO HAS CEASED FROM HIS OWN WORKS, AS GOD DID FROM HIS.

Hebrews 4:10

I AM WHAT I AM

First, kings of old used signets or rings that when pressed in hot wax, would seal a document, making it the law of the land. The king's seal was a very powerful instrument and it could not be broken by anyone but the king. The Bible refers to this type of seal in the book of Revelation when the Lord breaks open the seven seals.

Secondly, the term sealed is used in canning vegetables, etc. The cap is placed over the opening of the jar and sealed with paraffin (a type of wax) to prevent air from entering into the jar and contaminating the contents.

Thirdly, the term sealed is used in storage of perishable goods. If any of you have ever bought mail-order meat, you know that the food comes in a vacuum-packed container, like for canning, to preserve and protect the contents from contaminants entering inside.

Therefore, your spirit has been sealed, protected, and preserved from the corruption in this world, and no one can break this seal. Now that I've given you illustrations of this truth, let's examine what the Bible says to support these statements:

- *In whom you also trusted, after that you heard the word of truth, the gospel of your salvation. In whom also after that you believed, you were sealed with that holy Spirit of promise.* [Ephesians 1:13]

- *Whosoever abides in him sins not. Whosoever sins has not seen him, neither known him.* [1 John 3:6]

- *He that commits sin is of the devil; for the devil sinned from the beginning. For this purpose the Son of God was manifested, that*

AND I GIVE UNTO THEM ETERNAL LIFE; AND THEY SHALL NEVER PERISH, NEITHER SHALL ANY MAN PLUCK THEM OUT OF MY HAND.

John 10:28

he might destroy the works of the devil. Whosoever is born of God does not commit sin; for his seed remains in him. And he cannot sin, because he is born of God. [1 John 3:8-9]

So, you ask, does this mean that I believe the Bible supports the "Once saved, always saved" doctrine?

My answer is unequivocally "No." While we have been sealed by the Spirit of God until the day of redemption, the Bible teaches that it is possible to fall from grace. In Galatians 5:2-5, the apostle Paul wrote: _If you are circumcised, Christ shall profit you nothing. For I testify again to every man that is circumcised, that he is a debtor to do the whole law. Christ is become of no effect unto you, whosoever of you are justified by the law; you are fallen from grace. For we through the Spirit wait for the hope of righteousness by faith._

What Paul was teaching is that the Galatian church had received Christ and the Spirit by faith, but had since gone back into Judaism and works, which is by the flesh (circumcision). Therefore, it is possible for a person who was truly born again, to reject the gospel and fall from grace.

One may now ask, what if a person who was truly born again, went for a time and fell away due to unbelief, and now is being led back by the Spirit? Can this person be restored?

My answer is "Yes." Many well-meaning Christians have taken the following verses of scripture out of context:

- _For if we sin willfully after that we have received the knowledge of the truth, there remains no more sacrifice for sins._ [Hebrews

THIS ONLY WOULD I LEARN OF YOU, HAD YOU RECEIVED THE SPIRIT BY THE WORKS OF THE LAW, OR BY THE HEARING OF FAITH?

Galatians 3:2

10:26]

This scripture confirms the truths I discussed before in that your salvation was done in your spirit, and consequently, you cannot sin. But if your spirit did sin, you could not be saved because there remains no more sacrifice for sins.

This verse ties in directly with the verse from Hebrews 6 (below). The important part of this verse is *after we have received knowledge of the truth.* This indicates a level of maturity in Christ, which after knowing the full truth, we reject the gospel, we would fall from grace.

- *For it is impossible for those who were once enlightened, and have tasted of the heavenly gift, and were made partakers of the Holy Ghost, and have tasted the good word of God, and the powers of the world to come, if they shall fall away, to renew them again unto repentance; seeing they crucify themselves the Son of God afresh, and put him to an open shame.* [Hebrews 6: 4-6]

Many Christians whom had been in Christ for a number of years, have stumbled over this passage because of misunderstanding exactly what verses 4 and 5 mean. Again, this illustrates a great level of maturity on the part of the believer, not only in demonstrating the power of God, but in experiencing the world to come. However, maturity isn't the most important part of this passage. Rather what's important is the phrase, *to renew them again unto repentance.*

If a person, regardless of what he or she has done, is still feeling

BEING CONFIDENT OF THIS VERY THING, THAT HE WHICH HAS BEGUN A GOOD WORK IN YOU WILL PERFORM IT UNTIL THE DAY OF JESUS CHRIST.

Philippians 1:6

the conviction of their conscience and the drawing of the Holy Spirit back to Christ, then these verses do not apply to them, because it is impossible for the person this passage is describing to be truly repentant.

If you read in Romans 1 where Paul writes about God giving people over to vile affections and a reprobate mind, this is an illustration of an unrepentant heart. These folks are those who, as Paul wrote in Romans 1:32, *knowing the judgment of God, that they which commit such things are worthy of death, not only do the same, but have pleasure in them that do them.*

There may be some of you who have friends or loved ones who have fallen away from the faith, and the devil has lied to you, quoting Hebrews 6, saying that they are destined for hell. This is what the word of God says—that if they have a repentant heart, they are still eligible for God's grace.

THE LORD IS NOT SLACK CONCERNING HIS PROMISE, AS SOME MEN COUNT SLACKNESS; BUT IS LONG-SUFFERING TO US-WARD, NOT WILLING THAT ANY SHOULD PERISH, BUT THAT ALL SHOULD COME TO REPEN-TANCE.

2 Peter 3:9

8
Spirit vs. Flesh

This I say then, Walk in the Spirit and you shall not fulfill the lust of the flesh.
GALATIANS 5:16

In the life of a Christian, there is a constant battle raging between what the Bible calls the flesh, which, in this context, comprises of your mind, emotions, and body; and the spirit, which is the part of you that has been transformed into the image of Christ. As I discussed before, when you were born again, the only aspect of you that changed was your spirit. When your old sinful nature was crucified, it left behind not only a body, but also a mind that was programmed by the sinful nature.

Most Christians have been taught that what the apostle Paul wrote in his letter to the Romans concerning the struggle between the flesh and spirit (Romans 7) is a reflection of the true Christian life—and that even Paul struggled with carnal desires during his ministry. This is simply not true.

Rather, what we know as the 7th chapter of Romans is a reflection of two aspects of life: one, prior to being born again, and the other, when a Christian attempts to live according to the law and not grace. And this is what I want to discuss in this chapter.

Because a popular translation of the Bible (NIV) uses the term *sinful nature* in certain places when describing the flesh (as written in the King James Version) many Christians have been misled concerning what occurred at the new birth, and also what the Christian life is all about. The term *sinful nature* is not totally incorrect when used in the NIV, but in the context of describing someone who is born again, it is not correctly used. For example, Paul writes, *For when we were controlled by the sinful nature, the sinful passions aroused by the law were at work in our bodies, so that we bore fruit for death.* [Romans 7:5 NIV]

In this context, describing our nature prior to being born again as sinful is correct. The Bible says that before being a new creature, we were, by nature, children of wrath, and therefore, under the control and dominion of sin, which was given power by the law (Ephesians 2:3; Romans 7:1; 1 Corinthians 15:56). But now, in Christ, the old sinful nature (described as the "old man") was crucified with Christ, and is dead, having been replaced by *the new man which, after God, is created in righteousness and true holiness.* [Ephesians 4: 24] (see also Colossians 3:9-10)

The context where the NIV is incorrect, however, occurs in Romans 7:18, where the apostle Paul, as a Christian, is contrasting who he is in the spirit versus the flesh: *I know that nothing good lives in me, that*

BUT YOU ARE NOT IN THE FLESH, BUT IN THE SPIRIT, IF SO BE THAT THE SPIRIT OF GOD DWELL IN YOU. NOW IF ANY MAN HAVE NOT THE SPIRIT OF CHRIST, HE IS NONE OF HIS.

Romans 8:9

is, in my sinful nature. In this context, translating what Paul refers to as his flesh (KJV) or the part of him that has not been born again (i.e. his body and unrenewed mind) as being the *sinful nature* is not consistent to what Paul taught previously in Romans 6:6, *For we know that our old self was crucified with him so that the body of sin might be done away with, that we should no longer be slaves to sin.* [NIV]

Either the old man, the old sinful nature was crucified and is now dead and gone, or the Bible teaches that we are in essence schizo-phrenic—possessing two natures. And this is the crux of the problem of understanding what occurred at the new birth. Did the old sinful nature—the nature that compelled you to sin—die with Christ when you were born again? Or, do we have two natures that are constantly at war against the other to see who will dominate?

The apostle Paul was so very sure about this truth and knew the issue would come up that he stressed this very point when respond-ing to the question about continuing to live in sin: *How shall we, who are dead to sin, live any longer therein? Do you not know that so many of us as were baptized into Jesus Christ were baptized into his death? Therefore we are buried with him by baptism into death; that like as Christ was raised up from the dead by the glory of the Father, even so we also should walk in newness of life. For if we have been planted together in the likeness of his death, we shall be also in the likeness of his resurrec-tion. Knowing this, that our old man is crucified with him, that the body of sin might be destroyed, that henceforth we should not serve sin.* [Romans 6:2-6]

> FOR THOUGH HE WAS CRUCIFIED THROUGH WEAKNESS, YET HE LIVES BY THE POWER OF GOD. FOR WE ALSO ARE WEAK IN HIM, BUT WE SHALL LIVE WITH HIM BY THE POWER OF GOD TOWARD YOU.
>
> *2 Cor. 13:4*

When we use words like being dead, death, crucified, destroyed, and buried, it is conclusive that whatever we are describing no longer lives. Therefore, the sinful nature we were born with, is dead and gone, crucified and buried, and like as Christ was raised up from the dead, our nature has been resurrected anew by the Spirit of God through the new birth.

Because the NIV is so popular among Christians today, it is easy to see why people still see themselves as sinners instead of how God sees them in Christ as being righteous and holy. Furthermore, it is also easy to see why many Christians are not yet experiencing the freedom and victory the Lord Jesus died to give them—because they have yet to understand what occurred when they were born again.

What this deception has done is to create an excuse for the Christian when he or she fails. Teaching that, as a Christian, you still possess a sinful nature, only supports a passive and defeated way of thinking that as the Bible teaches brings forth death (Romans 8:6). Under this mindset, it is no wonder many Christians laboriously struggle with sin, sickness, depression, poverty, etc. Because as they have been taught, this is the way it should be. And when they get to Romans 8—the chapter that illustrates the victorious life in Christ—they are confused because this is not a reflection of how their lives are.

The belief that, as Christians, we continue to possess a sinful nature rips at the very fabric of the gospel and what the New Testament teaches concerning the new creature in Christ. Again, the

FOR YOU WERE SOMETIMES DARKNESS, BUT NOW ARE YOU LIGHT IN THE LORD. WALK AS CHILDREN OF LIGHT. FOR THE FRUIT OF THE SPIRIT IS IN ALL GOODNESS AND RIGHTEOUSNESS AND TRUTH.

Ephesians 5:8-9

apostle Paul, under the inspiration of the Spirit of God, adamantly stressed that in order to walk in the newness of life (Romans 6:4) we must first know that our old man is crucified, dead, buried, and no longer lives in us (v. 6).

Now that I have addressed this deception, let us move on to the true purpose for what was written in Romans 7—and that is to discourage the Christian from living according to the law instead of grace.

Grace vs. the Law

For sin shall not have dominion over you; for you are not under the law, but under grace. [Romans 6:14]

Without a foundational understanding of the new creature, it is easy to see how a person can read Romans 7 and conclude that Paul is describing the struggle of the Christian life. When we look at our natural lives and see that we still have many of the same fleshly desires and really haven't changed much since we were born again, these passages make a seemingly perfect fit for justifying what we realize in the natural.

We rationalize, "If the apostle Paul still struggled with sin—so much that he said, *'For that which I do, I allow not; for what I would, that do I not; but what I hate, that I do. For the good that I would, I do not; and the evil which I would not, that I do. Now if I do that I would not, it is no more I that do it, but sin that dwells in me.'* [Romans 7:15, 19-20] then why should I not have the same struggle?"

WHEREFORE IF YOU ARE DEAD WITH CHRIST FROM THE RUDIMENTS OF THE WORLD, WHY, AS THOUGH LIVING IN THE WORLD, ARE YOU SUBJECT TO ORDINANCES?

Colossians 2:20

I blame this line of thinking mostly on the church's failure to spiritually discern the truths of the word of God, but part of the blame lies in the way the Bible has been broken down and divided into chapters and verses. Because most of us in the western world are taught that paragraphs, sections, and chapters are used to separate different points of contention (either using paragraphs and/or sections to support a variety of sub-points) in order to improve clarity of thought and understanding, we view the Bible in the same way.

For example, we read different chapters of Romans and do not take into account that the apostle Paul did not dictate it this way—to be divided into chapters and verses. What we call the Book of Romans is actually a single letter written from a person to a group of people, specifically the Christian believers in Rome, but in a broad sense, to the entire church of Christ. It is one letter containing several teachings, issues, and questions; and was not the intent of its writer to divide and sub-divide it into parts, chapters, or verses.

However, in order to assist in applying scriptural references and making memorization easier, chapters and verses were added. It is because of these divisions that many Christians distinguish the teachings of one chapter from another, which I believe, is the cause of much of the misunderstanding and confusion in studying the Bible.

Many of us read the Bible at night and after reading for a certain length of time, as with any other book, we find an "appropriate" place to stop, which usually occurs at the end or beginning of a new

NOW THE LORD IS THAT SPIRIT; AND WHERE THE SPIRIT OF THE LORD IS, THERE IS LIBERTY.

2 Cor. 3:17

I AM WHAT I AM

chapter. I have to admit that whoever succeeded in creating these divisions did a very good job for the most part as it is evident that most of the divisions are made when a change of topic or point occurs. However, this isn't always true—especially in the context of what I am teaching about Romans 7. This is one of the reasons I believe that Romans 7 is so misunderstood—because many of us have failed to consider that the information contained in Romans 7 is directly related to what was taught in previous chapters—and specifically the latter part of chapter 6.

In essence, chapters 6 and 7 of Romans are teaching the very same principle. While in Romans 6: 1-11, Paul is teaching about the new creature and how we are dead to sin and alive unto God, the second part of this teaching (vv. 12-23) refers to whom we serve now in the newness of life, which is actually a manifestation of an understanding of this teaching. In other words, whom we serve in Christ is a fruit of understanding that we are dead to sin and alive unto God. This is why Paul writes, (I have transposed the order of the words for clarity) *Therefore* (or because of what he just wrote) *do not let sin reign in your mortal body, that you should obey it in the lusts thereof. Neither yield your members as instruments of unrighteousness unto sin; but yield yourselves unto God, as those that are alive from the dead, and your members as instruments of righteousness unto God. For sin shall not have dominion over you; for you are not under the law, but under grace.* [Romans 6:12-14]

There are two key points Paul wants to convey here. One, he

FOR AS MANY AS ARE OF THE WORKS OF THE LAW ARE UNDER THE CURSE. FOR IT IS WRITTEN, CURSED IS EVERY ONE THAT CONTINUES NOT IN ALL THINGS WHICH ARE WRITTEN IN THE BOOK OF THE LAW TO DO THEM.

Galatians 3:10

again stresses being dead to sin and alive unto God (*as those that are alive from the dead*) and that we should not yield our bodies to temptations and lusts as a result of the residue of the sinful nature's effects on our minds. But rather, we should yield ourselves as instruments of righteousness unto God. The second key point Paul makes actually prefaces what he is getting ready to teach in Romans 7—and this is the effect of living under the law instead of grace.

When we yield ourselves unto God as those who are alive from the dead (walking in the newness of life), and yielding our members as instruments of righteousness unto God, we are displaying the fruit of living under grace. Paul is making a contrast here in that if sin has dominion over you, you are not living under grace, but under the law. He made a similar statement in his letter to the Galatians, *This I say then, Walk in the Spirit and you shall not fulfill the lust of the flesh. For the flesh lusts against the Spirit, and the Spirit against the flesh; and these are contrary the one to the other; so that you cannot do the things that you would. But if you are led of the Spirit, you are not under the law.* [Galatians 5:16-18]

If you compare Romans 6:12-14 to Galatians 5:16-18, you will find that they teach the very same thing. Living by the law will cause sin to have dominion over you. Conversely, living according to grace (or walking in the Spirit) you will not fulfill the desires of the flesh. Why? *For the law of the Spirit of life in Christ Jesus has made me free from the law of sin and death.* [Romans 8:2]

Again, I must stress this point. Sin derives its power from the

I AM WHAT I AM

law, and as long as one seeks to live according to the law, sin will dominate his life. This is why it is impossible for a truly born again believer to have a sinful nature—because if he did, he would never be truly free from sin as the Scripture teaches. The Lord Jesus said, *And you shall know the truth, and the truth shall make you free.* [John 8:32] In order to be truly free, you must embrace the truth of who you are in Christ.

In verses 15-20 of Romans 6, Paul teaches that by yielding to sin, we are actually giving place to sin and subjection of the author of sin—the devil. And again, he reminds them of what had already occurred at the new birth, *But God be thanked, that you <u>were the servants of sin</u>, but you have obeyed from the heart that form of doctrine which was delivered you. <u>Being then made free from sin, you became the servants of righteousness</u>.* [Romans 6:17-18]

I pray you are connecting the language Paul uses in these passages and applying it to what is revealed in Romans 7. Being a servant of sin means you are being a servant of the law of sin and death—and not of grace. *But now being made free from sin, and become servants to God, you have your fruit unto holiness, and the end everlasting life. For the wages of sin is death; but the gift of God is eternal life through Jesus Christ our Lord.* [Romans 6:22-23]

And finally we get to Romans 7 where Paul continues this teaching on being a servant of the law and of sin. This time, he simply uses another application to being a servant; and here, he specifically addresses a certain group of people *Do you not know, brethren (for I*

> LIKEWISE RECKON ALSO YOURSELVES TO BE DEAD INDEED UNTO SIN, BUT ALIVE UNTO GOD THROUGH JESUS CHRIST OUR LORD.
>
> *Romans 6:11*

speak to them that know the law) how that the law has dominion over a man as long as he lives? [Romans 7:1]

Then Paul illustrates the bondage and obedience to the law as being similar to how a woman is bound by the law to her husband (Romans 7:2-3). Once again, Paul reminds us of what occurred at the new birth—being dead to the law of sin and being joined (baptized or married) into Christ—that we should walk in the newness of life. *Wherefore, my brethren, you also are become dead to the law by the body of Christ; that you should be married to another, even to him who is raised from the dead, that we should bring forth fruit unto God.* [Romans 7:4]

TELL ME, YOU THAT DESIRE TO BE UNDER THE LAW, DO YOU NOT HEAR THE LAW?

Galatians 4:21

This is the point the Scripture is trying to make—to discourage a Christian from going back to a life under the dominion of the law. The only way the apostle Paul can make an accurate illustration and comparison of what happens when a Christian attempts to live by the law is to describe the plight of a person outside the grace of God. If you read the latter half of Romans 6 and Romans 7 and compare them to Paul's letter to the Galatians, you will see that they mirror each other perfectly. The Galatians were being seduced into turning from the grace of God back to the weak and beggarly elements of the law where again they would be in bondage (Galatians 4:9).

This deception of so-called Jewish Christians was nothing new to Paul and the rest of his ministry. These deceivers were his greatest foes, and also the greatest enemies to the gospel of Christ. However, since Paul's letter to the Romans is considered the most comprehensive teaching on the gospel, it is no surprise that this warning is included.

Paul begins this comparison in verse 5 of Romans 7 and this is one time where the NIV Bible correctly interpreted what Paul wrote and the King James did not. The NIV says, *For when we were controlled by the sinful nature, the sinful passions aroused by the law were at work in our bodies, so that we bore fruit for death.* The King James translates this passage *For when we were in the flesh*, which is true as long as we understand this truth from Romans 8:9 *But you are not in the flesh, but in the Spirit, if so be that the Spirit of God dwells in you. Now if any man have not the Spirit of Christ, he is none of his.*

The harmony of the Bible teaches that we <u>had</u> (past tense) a sinful nature and we had flesh before we were born again. We still have flesh and an unrenewed mind, but, in Christ, we no longer have a sinful nature, but a newly created godly nature that is righteous and holy.

More accurately, the NIV translates that before being born again (again the only way Paul can illustrate this truth is to describe the bondage sin has over a non-believer) we were controlled by the sinful nature, and it was this sinful nature (empowered by the law) that compelled us to sin. In the same way, a Christian who is living according to the law, is being controlled by sin through the law—not a sinful nature. And this is what Paul is describing in Romans 7:7-20.

However, Paul prefaces the effects of living by the law by writing, *But now we are delivered from the law, that being dead wherein we*

> WHEREFORE, MY BRETHREN, YOU ALSO ARE BECOME DEAD TO THE LAW BY THE BODY OF CHRIST.
>
> *Romans 7:4*

were held, that we should serve in newness of spirit, and not in the oldness of the letter. [Romans 7:6] Once again, Paul reminds us that we have been delivered from the law of sin and death, and are dead to it and the bondage it provided, and that we should walk in the truth of the new creature as illustrated under the new covenant through the law of the Spirit of life in Christ Jesus.

After illustrating the effects of the bondage of living under the law, Paul foreshadows the only alternative to this bondage, *For I delight in the law of God after the inward man.* [Romans 7:22] Then he summarizes the war of the Spirit versus the flesh. *But I see another law in my members, warring against the law of my mind, and bringing me into captivity to the law of sin which is in my members. O wretched man that I am! Who shall deliver me from the body of this death? I thank God through Jesus Christ our Lord. So then with the mind I myself serve the law of God; but with the flesh the law of sin.* [Romans 7:23-25]

These last verses accurately express the war of the Spirit and flesh—in that it occurs in your mind, of which is manifested through your flesh. The Bible teaches that your mind controls what your body will do. If you are spirit minded, then you will not fulfill the desires of the flesh. But if you are fleshly minded, you are submitting to the bondage of the law of sin. *For they that are after the flesh do mind the things of the flesh; but they that are after the Spirit the things of the Spirit. For to be carnally minded is death; but to be spiritually minded is life and peace.* [Romans 8:5-6]

I AM WHAT I AM

In conclusion, we must go back to whom Paul is addressing at the beginning of Romans 7—those who know the law. He is simply continuing the teaching of being dead to sin and servants of righteousness. Romans 7 can be a true representation of the Christian life—as long as you intend on living according to the law. But as Paul cautioned in his letter to the Galatians, *Christ has become of no effect unto you, whosoever of you are justified by the law; you are fallen from grace.* [Galatians 5:4]

As I said before, many Christians view their lives as being reflective of what Romans 7 says, but this is because I believe so very few have heard the true gospel and are living under grace. I see and hear many Christians struggling with trying to live holy lives filled with frustration and anguish because they can never measure up to holiness in their flesh. And this is what the Lord wants to teach through the gospel—that you will come to the end of yourselves and submit to the grace and righteousness of God imparted to you when you are born again.

The victory described in Romans 8 is the true victory we have in Christ Jesus, and it should be an accurate reflection of our lives as long as we live according to grace—not as a license to sin, but as the *only* way to destroy the power and bondage of sin. It is only when you receive true revelation of the grace of God—the gospel—that you will begin to see the fruit of holiness it produces. I know this from personal experience that when you get a revelation of the grace of God and begin to live by it, you will see the verse from Galatians

> LIKEWISE RECKON ALSO YOURSELVES TO BE DEAD INDEED UNTO SIN, BUT ALIVE UNTO GOD THROUGH JESUS CHRIST OUR LORD.
>
> *Romans 6:11*

5:16 come true before your eyes. Fleshly desires that once held you captive will disappear as it is written, *This I say then, Walk in the Spirit and you shall not fulfill the lust of the flesh.* [Galatians 5:16]

Unfortunately, many Christians have been taught that "walking in the Spirit" means to live in obedience to God's law. This is simply not true. The Scripture teaches the obedience to God's law is a fruit of walking in the Spirit, which according to Romans 8:2 that *the law of the Spirit of life in Christ Jesus has made me free from the law of sin and death.* Let me remind you that the law is what gave sin its power and control over you, and if you attempt to live according to God's law, you will not only fall back under its dominion and control, but you will also put yourself back under the curse as it is written, *For as many as are of the works of the law are under the curse, for it is written, Cursed is every one that continues not in all things which are written in the book of the law to do them.* [Galatians 3:10] Therefore, "walking in the Spirit" is the same as walking and continuing in the grace of God.

Furthermore, the Bible teaches that *the law is good, if a man use it lawfully. Knowing this, that the law is not made for a righteous man, but for the lawless and disobedient, for the ungodly and for sinners, for unholy and profane, for murderers of fathers and murderers of mothers, for manslayers, for whoremongers, for them that defile themselves with mankind, for menstealers, for liars, for perjured persons, and if there be any other thing that is contrary to sound doctrine, according to the glorious gospel of the blessed God, which was committed to my trust.* [1

FOR I THROUGH THE LAW AM DEAD TO THE LAW, THAT I MIGHT LIVE UNTO GOD.

Galatians 2:19

I AM WHAT I AM

Timothy 1:8-11]

Combined with Paul's teaching in his letter to the Galatians as it is written, *But before faith came, we were kept under the law, shut up unto the faith which should afterwards be revealed. Wherefore the law was our schoolmaster to bring us unto Christ, that we might be justified by faith. But after that faith is come, we are no longer under a schoolmaster. For you are all the children of God by faith in Christ Jesus.* [Galatians 3:23-26]

And because the Scripture teaches that we are made righteous by faith (Romans 3:22) we no longer have to live according to God's law; and if you do, then you are nullifying the grace of God and empowering the bondage of sin in your body. This is the gospel, my brothers and sisters. When you live according to grace (walking in the Spirit) you will find yourself living a holier life than when you were trying to live according to the law.

FOR WHEN WE WERE IN THE FLESH, THE MOTIONS OF SINS, WHICH WERE BY THE LAW, DID WORK IN OUR MEMBERS TO BRING FORTH FRUIT UNTO DEATH.

Romans 7:5

God is not a man that he should lie; neither the son of man that he should repent. Has he said, and shall he not do it? Or has he spoken, and shall he not make it good? Behold, I have received commandment to bless; and he has blessed; and I cannot reverse it. He has not beheld iniquity in Jacob; neither has he seen perverseness in Israel. The LORD his God is with him; and the shout of a king is among them... Surely there is no enchantment against Jacob, neither is there any divination against Israel. According to this time is shall be said of Jacob and of Israel, What has God wrought!

NUMBERS 23:19-21, 23

PART III

Look in the Mirror

But we all, with open face beholding as in a glass the glory of the Lord, are changed into the same image from glory to glory, even as by the Spirit of the Lord.
2 CORINTHIANS 3:18

Behold, what manner of love the Father has bestowed upon us, that we should be called the sons of God. Therefor the world knows us not, because it knew him not.

Beloved, now are we the sons of God, and it does not yet appear what we shall be; but we know that, when he shall appear, we shall be like him; for we shall see him as he is.

And every man that has this hope in him purifies himself even as he is pure.

Whosoever commits sin transgresses also the law; for sin is the transgression of the law.

And you know that he was manifested to take away our sins; and in him is no sin.

Whosoever abides in him sins not. Whosoever sins has not seen him, neither known him.

Little children, let no man deceive you. He that does righteousness is righteous, even as he is righteous.

He that commits sin is of the devil; for the devil sinned from the beginning. For this purpose the Son of God was manifested, that he might destroy the works of the devil.

Whosoever is born of God does not commit sin; for his seed remains in him. And he cannot sin, because he is born of God.

In this the children of God are manifest, and the children of the devil. Whosoever does not righteousness is not of God, neither he that loves not his brother.

—1 John 3:1-10

Is a Christian a Sinner?

Do you yourselves not know how that Jesus Christ is in you except you be reprobates?
2 CORINTHIANS 13:5

While considering why many Christians continue to view themselves as sinners, the Lord gave me a profound question to ask: Does a butterfly walk around claiming that he is just a "glorified caterpillar"? Of course he doesn't. Because of his transformation, he is a butterfly and now he flies around giving beauty and life to the world instead of before, when as a caterpillar, he crawled on the ground devouring anything in its path.

There are four reasons many Christians see themselves as sinners. I call them "HIDERs" after the effects of original sin—when Adam and Eve tried to *hide* from God: Hardness of Heart, Immaturity, Deception, and Rebellion. All of them are involved, to different extents, in every person who makes this claim.

Hardness of Heart

This I say therefore, and testify in the Lord, that you henceforth walk not as other Gentiles walk, in the vanity of their mind, having the understanding darkened, being alienated from the life of God through the ignorance that is in them, because of the blindness of their heart. [Ephesians 4:17-18]

TAKE HEED, BRETHREN, LEST THERE BE IN ANY OF YOU AN EVIL HEART OF UNBE- LIEF, IN DEPARTING FROM THE LIVING GOD.

Hebrews 3:12

A great part of the apostle Paul's teachings warned us about not being ignorant of the things of God—and also concerning Satan's devices. To the Christian, ignorance is a result of two things: ignorance due to deception or immaturity, which I will cover in the next sections; or ignorance due to a hardened heart.

Most people associate the term "hardened heart" as being cold, calloused, unfeeling, or insensitive. As we will also see in the section on rebellion, most Christians would not claim that their hearts were hardened toward God. However, the Bible teaches that when a person is having a difficult time understanding spiritual truths, one of the reasons is because their heart is hardened.

In order to build calluses on your hands, you must work them over a period of time. The same is true for a hardened heart. It doesn't become hardened overnight, but has to be cultivated through a number of sources—mostly through unbelief. The Bible states that the heart can "wax" cold, referring to the traditional method of making candles. Traditionally, candles were made by extending a wick and submerging it into hot wax, removing it and allowing it to cool and harden. Then, once the first layer was hardened, it would be dipped

I AM WHAT I AM

again, adding another layer and so on until it achieved the desired thickness. This "waxing" as referred to in the Bible is the same way our heart becomes hardened. Fortunately, and unfortunately, our hearts, as with a candle, do not become hardened very quickly; and conversely, a hard heart does not soften overnight either.

Probably the greatest example in the Bible of a person with a hardened heart was Pharoah. In spite of witnessing miracle after miracle, he was still blind to the truth. This is what a hardened heart will do to a person—it will make you blind and deaf to the truth.

We have an instance in the Bible where Jesus taught concerning hardness of heart. In Mark 8, the Lord had just rebuked the Pharisees for seeking a sign from Him. After getting back into a ship, the Lord warned the disciples against the leaven of the Pharisees and of Herod. To further establish the context of this event, we see that in the span of probably only a few weeks prior, the Lord had fed 5,000 men with five loaves and two fishes (Mark 6:38); and He had fed 4,000 men with seven loaves and a few fishes (Mark 8:5). As the scripture reveals, the disciples were unable to understand what the Lord was saying because their hearts were hardened.

And they reasoned among themselves, saying, It is because we have no bread.

And when Jesus knew it, he said unto them, Why do you reason, because you have no bread? Do you still not perceive, neither understand? Is your heart still hardened? Having eyes, you see not? And having ears, you hear not? And do you not remember? [Mark 8:16-18]

AND I, BRETHREN, COULD NOT SPEAK UNTO YOU AS UNTO SPIRITUAL, BUT AS UNTO CARNAL, EVEN AS UNTO BABES IN CHRIST.

1 Cor. 3:1

Matthew's account of the same event adds some additional clarity to the exchange: *How is it that you do not understand that I spoke it not to you concerning bread, that you should beware of the leaven of the Pharisees and of the Sadducees?* [Matthew 16:11]

Most of us have wondered how the disciples could have been so spiritually dull. Wasn't it very clear to us that the Lord was talking about the Pharisees, and not bread? While the disciples were focused on their immediate circumstances, they failed to understand spiritual truth. Why?

Because their hearts were hardened. So, why were their hearts hardened? We find the answer in Mark 6 during the account of Jesus walking on the water. The disciples, after witnessing Jesus walk on water, *were sore amazed in themselves beyond measure, and wondered. For <u>they considered not the miracle of the loaves</u>. For their heart was hardened.* [Mark 6:51-52]

They had failed to remember that Jesus had performed many miracles prior to this event—and more recently, he had fed the 5,000 with five loaves. So, why would the disciples be sore amazed beyond measure, which translates in today's vernacular as "freaking out" when they saw Jesus walking on the water? Again, the answer is due to a hardened heart, which causes you to forget what the Lord has done in the past.

They were just like Pharoah, who seemed to have forgotten all the things that had come to pass through Moses. Why couldn't he just get it? Because his heart was hardened. Lest we find ourselves

I AM WHAT I AM

being overly critical of the disciples for their hard heartedness, we need to examine our own lives concerning our understanding of spiritual truth. Being hard hearted makes you spiritually retarded. And as you will see in a subsequent section, it plays a role as a deceived person is regarded as a forgetful hearer of the word.

Let's dig a little deeper into the teaching from Mark 6. Verse 45 says that the Lord had *constrained his disciples to get into the ship, and to go to the other side before unto Bethsaida, while he sent away the people.* The word constrained means to compel or force, which when interpreted correctly, we understand that the Lord had forced them into the ship. Have you ever wondered why Jesus had to force the disciples into the ship? We have to remember that four of them, Peter, Andrew, James, and John were professional fishermen. They knew the sea, and being fishermen for such a long time, they knew to watch the weather before embarking on a trip on the sea. The disciples knew there was a storm coming, and this is the reason Jesus had to compel them to get on the boat—especially knowing that Jesus was going to remain behind to send away the people.

Once on the sea the storm came, but did the disciples remember what Jesus had already done? No, instead of meditating (which is what "considering" means) on the miracle of the loaves, they toiled through the storm under their own strength. And when they saw Jesus walking on the sea, they thought it was a ghost. *For they all saw him, and were troubled.* (v. 50) Again I ask, why would the disciples, when fearing for their lives in the midst of a storm, be troubled

OUR FATHERS UNDERSTOOD NOT YOUR WONDERS IN EGYPT; THEY REMEMBERED NOT THE MULTITUDE OF YOUR MERCIES; BUT PROVOKED HIM AT THE SEA, EVEN AT THE RED SEA.

Psalm 106:7

by the presence of Jesus? Did they think He could or would not save them? It's true that the Bible says that Jesus would have passed them by had they not cried out to Him (v. 48). Wouldn't you have been glad to see Jesus? However, instead of being glad, they were afraid, supposing He was a ghost.

Because they had not considered, meditated, or thought strongly upon the great miracles that Jesus had performed, and recently in feeding approximately 15,000 people with five loaves of bread and two fish, their hearts had hardened.

FOR THIS PEOPLE'S HEART IS WAXED GROSS, AND THEIR EARS ARE DULL OF HEAR-ING, AND THEIR EYES THEY HAVE CLOSED...

Matthew 13:15

If you still see yourself as a sinner, then you have a hardened heart toward what God has done for you through the cross. You have failed to consider the miracle of the new creature; and conse-quently, your eyes, ears, and understanding are dull insomuch that you cannot perceive spiritual truth. There is no condemnation in this. I am not concluding that a person with a hardened heart to-ward God is not saved or in outright rebellion against God. It just means that this person's spiritual senses (faith) have been dulled so much that they have difficulty understanding spiritual truths.

The good news is that the Lord has given unto us His Spirit, by which we can know the things that are freely given to us by God (1 Corinthians 2:10). First and foremost, you must consider the miracle of salvation that has taken you from being a child of the devil and transforming you into a child of God.

In conclusion, I want to address the fact that our hearts can also be hardened through sin (Hebrews 3:8-19). The reason I didn't dis-

I AM WHAT I AM

cuss the effects of sin is because all of us know that sin affects our hearts. No one needs to remind us about sin. The reason I focus more on unbelief is because of its subtlety and likelihood to lead well-meaning Christians into destruction without them knowing it. Secondly, these verses of scripture do not indicate that the disciples were in sin while on the boat. Yes, I know that all unbelief is sin, fear is sin, etc., etc. But they weren't on the ship looking at pornography, getting drunk, or telling dirty jokes. They were trying to stay alive the best way they knew how. Once again I point to the subtlety of unbelief and how by meditating on the things in the natural instead of the things of God, your heart will become hardened just like the disciples.

Whatever you focus your mind on is what you will be sensitive to. If your thoughts are filled with things of the world, then you will be sensitive to the prince of this world. If you focus your mind on the things of God (to be Spirit minded), then you will be sensitive to God. The following verse from Romans 8:6 has virtually changed my life: *For to be carnally minded is death, but to be spiritually minded is life and peace.*

So, how do you soften your heart toward God? First, you begin meditating on the word of God—all day, every day. I'm not talking about spending five minutes reading the Bible and then going on with your day. Although if you spent your entire day meditating on one verse of scripture, your life would be dramatically changed.

Now you ask, "How can I do my job and think about God's word

YOU WILL KEEP HIM IN PERFECT PEACE, WHOSE MIND IS STAYED ON YOU; BECAUSE HE TRUSTS IN YOU.

Isaiah 26:3

at the same time?" How many of you go throughout the day, doing your job, but the predominant part of the day was spent thinking about some problem you were having—either with your spouse, boss, friend, family member? You were certainly able to do your job and think upon all the rotten things in your life. Most of you have even lost sleep because of some problem you're having, but would you be willing to stay up all night with God in His word and in prayer? Why can't you do the same with the word of God?

Most people would disagree with me, but the fact that our hearts can harden is a God-given trait. Have any of you seen or experienced a time when you were trying to get someone's attention (or they yours) and you or they were so focused on what they were doing, they didn't even hear what you said? This is a characteristic of having a hardened heart. God has created us with the ability to completely focus our attention, so that our minds are not distracted. However, God intended for this trait to be used to block out the corruption that is in the world. God wants us to harden ourselves to the world, where it will not cause us to be distracted.

I spent thirteen years as a police officer; and during my career, I witnessed many terrible things, which caused my heart to harden. When I saw a dead body for the first time, it affected me. But after seeing hundreds of dead bodies, some dismembered, burned, and riddled with stab wounds or bullet holes, I became more hardened with each incident. I was like the wick of the candle. Each time I was immersed in death, I became more hardened to it—layers upon lay-

I AM WHAT I AM

ers of death. This is why some children who kill can be so cold-hearted—because they have grown up witnessing death—either through television, movies, or video games.

Once you have begun focusing on the word of God, you must begin to destroy all the inroads of unbelief in your life. This includes most television, radio, books, and other worldly entertainment or amusement.

Some of you may know this, but the word "muse" means "to think, ponder, consider, mull over, etc." However, when you add the letter "a" to it, we get the word amuse. Most students of the English language know that when the letter "a" is used as a prefix, it means "not or without". For example, the adjective "moral" describes a person concerned with right and wrong. However, you add the prefix "a" to it, making the word "amoral" you get a person described to be without any sense of right or wrong. Consequently, when you are being "a-mused" you are in a state of not or without thought or consideration. The dictionary defines "amuse" as being a "pleasant diversion".

Many of you will scoff at this, but I challenge you to name five shows on television (other than Christian television) that lift up the name of Jesus. There aren't any, my brothers and sisters. If these shows aren't drawing you closer to the Lord, they are dragging you away. Someone will say, "Well, we have to live a balanced life. We can't just shelter ourselves from the world!"

The Bible says this: *I would have you wise unto that which is good,*

MY SON, ATTEND UNTO MY WISDOM, AND BOW YOUR EAR TO MY UNDER-STANDING.

Proverbs 5:1

and simple concerning that which is evil. [Romans 16:19] It is God's desire for us to be wise concerning His word and will for our lives, and although the Bible teaches us not to be ignorant of Satan's devices, we are not to be immersed in them for the sake of knowledge. Think about the candle and how it was hardened by frequent immersions in the hot wax. In other words, we are to be naïve concerning the evil in the world. Because if we bathe ourselves in the world, the natural consequences will be that we will think about those things.

For those of you who want to live a balanced life, let's look at the word balance. Balance, by definition, means to remain in equilibrium. In the context of this subject, living a balanced life means it is your desire to have an equal portion of God and an equal portion of the world—an equal portion of the word of God and an equal portion of the word of the devil and so on. This is what balanced is, brothers and sisters.

BUT YET I WOULD HAVE YOU WISE UNTO THAT WHICH IS GOOD, AND SIMPLE CONCERN-ING EVIL.

Romans 16:19

Immaturity

When I was a child, I spoke as a child, I understood as a child, I thought as a child. But when I became a man, I put away childish things. [1 Corinthians 13:11]

The second reason Christians fail to realize who they are in Christ is because of immaturity concerning their understanding of the word of God. The Bible teaches that spiritual truths can only be perceived by a man's spirit. Consequently, it is impossible for those who walk in the vanity of their minds (Ephesians 4:17) to ever understand the things of God.

The word of God is spirit (John 6:63), written under the direct inspiration of the Holy Spirit (2 Timothy 3:16) and therefore totally accurate and reliable. And yet, until we, by the Spirit, know what the words are saying, the Bible will not be profitable to us (Hebrews 4:2), which could explain why many people who "know" the scriptures and even have many of them memorized, are unable to walk in the victory the word was given to produce.

Another word for being spiritually immature is carnal. The word carnal means of the flesh, but in the context of scripture, not only does it pertain to the flesh, but it also means "of the senses."

Being carnal doesn't necessarily refer to sin; but rather is a reflection of the predominant thinking of a person, as in being carnally minded as opposed to being spiritually minded (Romans 8:6). To be carnally minded is to focus your thoughts on temporal things, or things of your five senses. While a person who is spiritually minded tends to focus on eternal things, the things of God, or the word of God.

The Bible teaches in Romans 8:6 that *to be carnally minded is death; but to be spiritually minded is life and peace.*

The Lord gave me revelation of the true meaning of this scripture and how it applies to our entire lives in Christ. Understanding it has changed my life. We'll talk more about this later, but if you can just understand this one truth: Our lives are governed by the

FOR WHEN FOR THE TIME YOU OUGHT TO BE TEACHERS, YOU HAVE NEED THAT ONE TEACH YOU AGAIN WHICH BE THE FIRST PRINCIPLES OF THE ORACLES OF GOD.

Hebrews 5:12

way we think. If you think about all the murder, poverty, hatred, greed, perversion in the world, then all you will have is death, despair, depression, etc. But if all you think about is the word of God and the things of God, all you will have is life, prosperity, health, and peace.

A Christian is carnal not because he is young in the Lord, but a Christian is carnal because he is influenced more by what he feels, sees, tastes, hears, or smells than what the word of God says. In fact, the newly born again Christian is often more likely to be more spirit minded than one who's "been in church" for many years. Unfortunately, many "mature" Christians believe they know it all when all they know is the superficial truths of the word of God.

Although he is truly born again and loves God, the carnal Christian's life is governed by the world, which explains why immaturity is a reason the Christian still sees himself as a sinner. He simply cannot understand spiritual truths because, as the Bible says, they are spiritually discerned. In fact, some of you may have already thought that the material in this book was foolish, which also reveals that you are carnal because spiritual truth is foolishness to the natural or carnal man.

Now we have received, not the spirit of the world, but the spirit which is of God, that we might know the things that are freely given to us of God. Which things also we speak, not in the words of man's wisdom teaches, but which the Holy Ghost teaches, comparing spiritual things with spiritual. But the natural man receives not the things of the Spirit of God; for they are foolishness unto him. Neither can he know them

BRETHREN, BE NOT CHILDREN IN UNDERSTANDING; HOWBEIT IN MALICE BE CHILDREN, BUT IN UNDERSTANDING BE MEN.

1 Cor. 14:20

I AM WHAT I AM

because they are spiritually discerned. [1 Corinthians 2:12-14]

Being and remaining a carnal Christian isn't entirely an individual's fault, although it is your own responsibility to grow in the grace and knowledge of our Lord Jesus Christ (2 Timothy 2:15, 2 Peter 3:18). For the most part, churches do not teach or walk in the full counsel of God. More than half of all churches in the United States are denominational churches, which have taken bits and pieces of the word of God and turned them into their church's doctrine. What's worse is that they proclaim it to be the true gospel of Jesus Christ! How can a church that doesn't do everything the Lord Jesus did and commissioned and empowered us to do (heal the sick, raise the dead, cast out devils, cleanse lepers, etc.) claim that they preach the complete gospel?

This illustration doesn't apply only to denominational churches, but also to ones that claim to be "non-denominational" but are actually denominational churches in disguise. The church of Jesus Christ is not subject to labels as if it were some marketing concept. Rather, the church is the functioning body of Christ that lives to be witnesses unto His resurrection, preaching the gospel with the Lord confirming the word with signs and wonders following (Mark 16:20).

This is why it is of utmost importance to commit yourself fully to what 2 Timothy 2:15 teaches: *Study to show yourself approved unto God, a workman that needs not to be ashamed, rightly dividing the word of truth.*

You do not need to be taught the word of God by your church or

THROUGH MIGHTY SIGNS AND WONDERS, BY THE POWER OF THE SPIRIT OF GOD; SO THAT FROM JERUSALEM, AND ROUND ABOUT UNTO ILYRICUM, I HAVE FULLY PREACHED THE GOSPEL OF CHRIST.

Romans 15:19

by man. In other words, you cannot live off the revelation of others without making revelation of God's word your own. God uses the Bible, preaching, and teaching to bring you revelation, which is given by the Spirit. The Bible says, *These things I have written unto you concerning them that seduce you. But the anointing which you have received of him abides in you, and you need not that any man teach you. But as the same anointing teaches you of all things, and is truth, and is no lie, and even as it has taught you, you shall abide in him.* [1 John 2:26-27]

EVER LEARNING, AND NEVER ABLE TO COME TO THE KNOWL-EDGE OF THE TRUTH.

2 Timothy 3:7

The Holy Spirit was given to us to lead us into all truth and to teach us all things (John 14:26; 16:13). It was not written for our intellectual comprehension only, but to the innermost part of our heart. This, I believe, is the chief reason many people have difficulty understanding the scriptures—because they are trying to understand it using only their limited brains. The word of God must inspire our heart before it can enlighten our mind.

- *And I, brethren, could not speak unto you as unto spiritual, but as unto carnal, even as unto babes in Christ.* [1 Corinthians 3:1]
- *Of whom (Jesus) we have many things to say, and are hard to be uttered, seeing you are dull of hearing. For when for the time you ought to be teachers, you have need that one teach you again which be the first principles of the oracles of God; and are become such as have need of milk, and not of strong meat. For every one that uses milk is unskillful in the word of righteousness, for he is a babe. But strong meat belongs to them that are*

I AM WHAT I AM

of full age, even those who by reason of use have their senses exercised to discern both good and evil. [Hebrews 5:11-14]

Deception

But be doers of the word, and not hearers only, <u>deceiving your ownselves</u>. For if any be a hearer of the word, and not a doer, he is like a man <u>looking at his natural face in a mirror</u>. For <u>he looks at himself</u>, and goes <u>his way</u>, and immediately forgets what manner of man he was. [James 1:22-24]

The third reason why Christians view themselves as sinners is because they are deceived. Let's go back to the garden of Eden where Adam and Eve caused the fall of the entire human race. Why had Eve sinned? What was her explanation? *And the woman said, The serpent beguiled me, and I did eat.* [Genesis 3:13]

The word *beguiled* in this context means to utterly deceive, which is what the devil accomplished with Eve. Let us remember that the deception was first in doubting what God had said concerning the tree, and then he questioned who God had said she was.

Now the serpent was more subtle than any beast of the field which the Lord God had made. And he said to the woman, Yea, has God said, You shall not eat of every tree of the garden?

And the woman said to the serpent, We may eat of the fruit of the trees of the garden. But of the fruit of the tree which is in the midst of the garden, God has said, You shall not eat of it, neither shall you touch it, lest you die.

TAKE HEED TO YOUR-SELVES, THAT YOUR HEART BE NOT DECEIVED, AND YOU TURN ASIDE, AND SERVE OTHER GODS, AND WORSHIP THEM.

Deut. 11:16

113

And the serpent said to the woman, You shall not surely die. For God does know that in the day you eat thereof, then your eyes shall be opened, and you shall be as gods, knowing good and evil.

And when the woman saw that the tree was good for food, and that it was pleasant to the eyes, and a tree to be desired to make one wise, she took of the fruit thereof, and did eat, and gave also to her husband with her; and he did eat. [Genesis 3:1-6]

What was Adam's sin? His sin was that he chose to listen to his wife over God. Oh, what a tangled web we weave when we listen to what man has said instead of what God has said. While Eve had been deceived, Adam had intentionally disobeyed. This is what deception can do to us. When we allow ourselves to be deceived—even by our Christian brothers and sisters, our pastors and teachers—we open the door to rebellion against God.

Let's go back to the parable of the eagle and examine the reason why he thought he was a chicken. Most would answer that if one were an eagle, or butterfly, and went around claiming they were something else, they were either ignorant or deceived. We know why the eagle was ignorant, but how had he been deceived? For his entire life, he lived as a chicken, was told he was a chicken by his eagle brothers, and even looked in a mirror to see that he looked like a chicken. All the time, a voice inside him was telling him something different. However, he chose to believe what he had been told by others and what he had seen in a distorted mirror.

This is what the scripture from James 1 is teaching—that if you

O, FOOLISH GALATIANS, WHO HAS BEWITCHED YOU, THAT YOU SHOULD NOT OBEY THE TRUTH, BEFORE WHOSE EYES JESUS CHRIST HAD BEEN EVIDENTLY SET FORTH, CRUCIFIED AMONG YOU?

Galatians 3:1

hear the word only and don't act upon it, then you have deceived yourself. This deceived person is like a man who looks at his natural face in a mirror, and when he looks at himself, he goes his own way, forgetting what manner of man (the word said) he was.

This is the root of the answer to the question why many Christians see themselves as sinners. First of all, they're looking at themselves instead of looking to Jesus, the author and finisher of our faith. Secondly, because they're looking in a natural mirror, they only see themselves in the flesh.

Rebellion

For they, being ignorant of God's righteousness, and going about to establish their own righteousness, have not submitted themselves unto the righteousness of God. For Christ is the end of the law for righteousness to every one that believes. [Romans 10:3-4]

As a hard heart makes a person vulnerable to deception, deception will often lead to rebellion. Most people would not consider it possible for a Christian to be in rebellion against God. They seem to contradict each other because once we are in Christ, we are no longer in rebellion against God. While this is true in a broad sense of our position prior to receiving the gift of salvation and reconciliation with God, there is a more subtle rebellion against what God has done to make us blameless in His sight.

Although this verse from Romans 10 was written concerning Israel, I believe it strikes to the very heart of why much of the body

YOU DID RUN WELL; WHO DID HINDER YOU THAT YOU SHOULD NOT OBEY THE TRUTH?

Galatians 5:7

of Christ has failed to realize who they truly are; and consequently, they are toiling in their own strength, trying to live a godly life, and failing miserably. The truth is that they, being ignorant or misinformed about God's righteousness, are going about to establish their own righteousness through good works, going to church, paying tithes, etc., and have clearly shown (by their own words) that they have not submitted to the righteousness of God.

There are well-meaning folks who sincerely believe—not consciously—that they received salvation by grace, but in order to keep it, they must perform good works or live holy lives. The verse from Philippians 2:12: *work out your own salvation with fear and trembling* is quoted to support this belief. This false teaching breeds the notion that a Christian goes throughout the day on a roller coaster ride of being saved, sinning and losing salvation, asking for forgiveness, being saved again, and over and over and over, day after day after day. Does this sound familiar?

There are others who don't take it to this extreme—that you lose your salvation through sin, but believe that sin still separates the Christian from God and that one loses his or her fellowship with the Lord when they sin. With this loss of fellowship, the person believes he also temporarily foreits the blessings of God as if God's blessing is based on our own performance.

And only when this person "prays through" or in other words, confesses his sins and is cleansed from all unrigheousness (an incorrect application of 1 John 1:9), will the relationship be restored, and be in "right standing" with God.

Although people who live by either of these philosophies would not admit it, they unconsciously begin to rate sins, thinking the "little sins" like speeding or telling a lie have no effect on our relationship with God. But "big sins" like adultery, murder, and not paying your tithes will either cause you to be in danger of hell, or at the very least, God will remove Himself from you because He can't fellowship with a dirty vessel.

Fortunately, the Bible doesn't teach this nonsense. While different sins have different consequences in the natural, God does not view sin in varying degrees as it is written: *For whosoever shall keep the whole law, and yet offend in one point, he is guilty of all. For he that said, Do not commit adultery, said also, Do not kill. Now if you commit no adultery, yet if you kill, you are become a transgressor of the law.* [James 2:10-11]

Sin isn't always something you do, but can be something you don't do. *Therefore to him that knows to do good, and does it not, to him it is sin.* [James 4:17]

By making salvation based upon what you do or don't do, is nullifying the grace of God. Short of rejecting Jesus as Savior, there is no sin that will send you to hell. Likewise, there is nothing you can do to earn your salvation. This attitude, my brothers and sisters, is rebellion against God in its most subtle form.

If you continue to focus your efforts in doing good works, trying to establish your own righteousness, you have failed to submit to

FOR IF, WHEN WE WERE ENEMIES, WE WERE RECONCILED TO GOD BY THE DEATH OF HIS SON, MUCH MORE BEING RECONCILED, WE SHALL BE SAVED BY HIS LIFE.

Romans 5:10

the righteousness of God. I think the apostle Paul said it best: *And be found in him, not having mine own righteousness, which is of the law, but that which is through the faith of Christ, the righteousness which is of God by faith.* [Philippians 3:9]

As I said before, this kind of rebellion is very subtle. I doubt anyone would admit they hadn't submitted to the righteousness of God, but their actions speak differently. When your actions indicate that you must "do" something (other than believe) either to keep your salvation or earn the acceptance of God through works, you are in essence, saying that the sacrifice of Jesus Christ and the gift of His righteousness was not enough to keep you saved. This is how the apostle Paul perceived the Galatian church:

I do not frustrate the grace of God. For if righteousness come by the law, then Christ is dead in vain. O foolish Galatians, who has bewitched you, that you should not obey the truth, before whose eyes Jesus Christ has been evidently set forth, crucified among you? This only would I learn of you, Have you received the Spirit by the works of the law, or by the hearing of faith? Are you so foolish? Having begun in the Spirit, are you now made perfect by the flesh? [Galatians 2:21-3:3]

So then you ask me, "Should we stop doing good works because it doesn't matter—that by seeking to do good works we are actually living by the law?"

Many of you will also quote from James 2:20, 26 that says *faith without works is dead.*

There is nothing wrong with seeking to do good works as long

I MARVEL THAT YOU ARE SO SOON REMOVED FROM HIM THAT CALLED YOU INTO THE GRACE OF CHRIST UNTO ANOTHER GOSPEL.

Galatians 1:6

I AM WHAT I AM

as God is given the glory for them, and they are done because you are motivated by God's kind of love (1 Corinthians 13:3). However, many have made good works and service a route of acceptance by the Lord instead of a fruit of knowing Him. Remember, holiness and good works are a "fruit" of the Spirit—not a route to it. As an apple tree doesn't have to try to bear apples, a Christian shouldn't have to try to do good works or live a holy life—it just happens as a result of his or her relationship with the Lord.

As James wrote, *Yea, a man may say, You have faith, and I have works. Show me your faith without your works, and I will show you my faith by my works.* [James 2:18]

These verses are teaching us that when we are born again, we take upon the nature of the Lord Jesus, *because as he is so are we in this world.* [1 John 4:17] Therefore, good works will be a byproduct of our relationship with God—a fruit of the Spirit. Jesus said it this way in John 7:38, *He that believes on me, as the scripture has said, out of his belly shall flow rivers of living water.*

Jesus didn't have to try to do good works; they were a fruit of being anointed by the Holy Spirit (Acts 10:38). By the same token, we should be doing the same works (and greater) as Jesus did (John 14:12); not because we are trying to earn the favor of God, or even to prove ourselves to be Christians; but because this is who we are as a result of having been anointed by the Holy Spirit as well.

As long as you seek to live by the righteousness of Jesus, and not according to you own performance, the Christian life should be easy.

BELOVED, BELIEVE NOT EVERY SPIRIT, BUT TRY THE SPIRITS WHETHER THEY ARE OF GOD, BECAUSE MANY FALSE PROPHETS ARE GONE OUT INTO THE WORLD.

1 John 4:1

NOT BY
WORKS OF
RIGHTEOUS
WHICH WE
HAVE DONE,
BUT
ACCORDING
TO HIS
MERCY HE
SAVED US,
BY THE
WASHING OF
REGENERA-
TION, AND
RENEWING
OF THE
HOLY
GHOST.

Titus 3:5

I cannot stress this enough. Our holiness isn't based on what we have done, are doing, or will do. Our holiness is based on what the Lord Jesus did on the cross. The apostle Paul defined the mystery of godliness in 1 Timothy 3:16: *And without controversy great is the mystery of godliness. God was manifest in the flesh, justified in the Spirit, seen of angels, preached unto the Gentiles, believed on in the world, received up into glory.*

Notice that in this confession, deeds of man (either good or bad) are not included. What Paul is telling us is that the mystery of godliness is none other than the Spirit of Christ Himself living inside the heart of every believer. Or better yet, *Christ in you, the hope of glory.* [Colossians 1:27]

As I said when I began this section, you may not consider yourself to be in rebellion against God, but hopefully, I have revealed the subtlety of this issue. If you are going about trying to remain saved through your own works, you have not submitted fully to the righteousness of God; and therefore, you are in rebellion against God. I don't say this to condemn or criticize you. I say this to encourage you to begin walking in the truth that has already, and will continue to keep you free (John 8:32).

Notwithstanding, I believe that rebellion in this manner—by making your righteousness and holiness dependent upon your own works—is the greatest offense to God, in that by considering your performance (either good or bad) above what Jesus suffered to give you His righteousness. Most Christians have failed to comprehend the exceedingly great value that God has placed on the suffering and ultimate sacrifice of His beloved Son. Otherwise, they would not try to live according to their own righteousness. God hates sin, and some sin is categorized as an abomination unto God, but the greatest sin pales in comparison to rejecting the free gift of salvation and righteousness by simply placing your trust in the Lord Jesus Christ.

The Bible says, *Submit yourselves therefore to God. Resist the devil and he will flee from you.* [James 4:7]

Many Christians interpret this scripture to be speaking about our obedience to God's commands. While I agree that in part it speaks about obedience, I tend to lay more weight to our level of submission to the extent of His redemptive work on the cross. This is why verse six speaks about God's incredible grace and that when we humbly accept His grace, without our own works, we will be able to completely resist the devil.

We just cannot get it through our heads that we don't have to do anything but receive the gift of salvation, righteousness, redemption, healing, deliverance, prosperity, and power and authority over the devil. Our performance mentality screams, "It's too good to be true! There must be a catch somewhere! We've got to do something in return!"

You're right, the gospel seems to be almost unbelievable because we have been taught since we were children that love and acceptance from others is based on our performance. God's love doesn't function this way. If it did, we would have reason to boast. However, the Bible

AND THIS IS HIS COMMANDMENT, THAT WE SHOULD BELIEVE ON THE NAME OF HIS SON JESUS CHRIST, AND LOVE ONE ANOTHER, AS HE GAVE US COMMANDMENT.

1 John 3:23

says, *For by grace you are saved through faith; and that not of yourselves. It is the gift of God. Not of works, lest any man boast.* [Ephesians 2:8-9]

While the devil has succeeded in deceiving much of the body of Christ in viewing themselves as sinners, he has also succeeded in a far greater way in bringing forth the same lies to the world through the theory of evolution. The Bible teaches that a sinner has no inheritance in the kingdom of God. Consequently, a sinner is no better than a highly-evolved ape. As I said before, it's the same strategy, but wrapped in a different package. If the devil, through what is taught in public schools, can blind the world to the truth of where human beings have come from, he has succeeded in blinding them to who they really are. In order to truly understand who we are, we must know from where we came, which is from God. Therefore, not only is it important to embrace our true identities in Christ, but also to comprehend from where we have come, and also where we are going. A full revelation and faith in these truths will result in the complete victory the Lord Jesus died to give us.

AND NO MARVEL; FOR SATAN HIMSELF IS TRANSFORMED INTO AN ANGEL OF LIGHT.

2 Cor. 11:14

10

The True Mirror

But whoever looks into the perfect law of liberty, and continues therein, he being not a forgetful hearer, but a doer of the work, this man shall be blessed in his deed.

James 1:25

Here is a profound truth: You have never seen your own face. Yes, you've seen your face in mirrors, photographs, and videos, but they are not your true face. The face you see in a mirror is a reflection. In photographs or videos, all you see are images or projections of light that with technology can be distorted greatly.

Despite this truth, you trust that what you see in a mirror or photograph is an exact representation of who you are. This can be proven when you see that your hair is messed up, or that something is on your face, you fix it. Or, when you see a picture of yourself, you may think, "I should lose some weight."

Similarly, you cannot see your brain, or any other internal organs, but you trust that you have them since you are able to live, breathe, and think. The same is true for your spirit. You cannot see your spirit; and since God is a Spirit, you cannot see Him with your eyes. However, you have a mirror by which you can see God and also see who you are in the spirit. This mirror is the living word of God. Just as you can look in a mirror to see your physical image, and trust it as being a true reflection of who you are in the flesh, you can look into the word of God, and trust that it is a true reflection of who you are in the spirit. Remember what the Lord Jesus said, *God is a Spirit* [John 4:24], His words are spirit (John 6:63), and those who are born again are spirit (John 3:6).

The Bible teaches that prior to being born again, a person is in bondage to sin through Old Testament law, (Romans 7; Galatians 3:23) which therefore causes a lost person to be blind and separated from the truth of the liberty in Christ Jesus. In his second letter to the Corinthians, the apostle Paul used the veil Moses had to wear after being in the presence of God (Exodus 34:29-32) to illustrate the difference between the old and new covenants. As long as a person is living according to the law—according to their own goodness and performance—they are separated from the glory of God; but when a person humbles himself and turns to the grace and righteousness provided by the Lord, the veil is removed and allows them to see the truth of the new covenant. Consequently, when we, with an unveiled face, (meaning when we believe the gospel) see the glory of the Lord Jesus as if we were looking in a mirror, we are changed into the same image, from glory to glory, as by the Spirit of the Lord, as the Scripture says.

And not as Moses, which put a veil over his face, that the children of

I AM WHAT I AM

Israel could not steadfastly look to the end of that which is abolished. But their minds were blinded. For until this day remains the same veil untaken away in the reading of the old testament, which veil is done away in Christ. But even unto this day, when Moses is read, the veil is upon their heart. Nevertheless when it shall turn to the Lord, the veil shall be taken away. Now the Lord is that Spirit; and where the Spirit of the Lord is, there is liberty. But we all, with open face beholding as in a glass the glory of the Lord, are changed into the same image from glory to glory, even as by the Spirit of the Lord. [2 Corinthians 3:13-18]

AND JESUS SAID, "FOR JUDGMENT I AM COME INTO THIS WORLD, THAT THEY WHICH SEE NOT MIGHT SEE; AND THAT THEY WHICH SEE MIGHT BE MADE BLIND."

John 9:39

What the apostle Paul is teaching is that now that the blindness (the veil) has been removed, you should see yourself as transformed into the image of Christ. Therefore, you cannot look at yourself in a natural mirror and expect to see who you are in Christ. A natural mirror is a reflection of who we are in the flesh. Rather, we must look at the image of Jesus revealed to us by the Spirit and through the written word of God. The scripture from James explains it further:

But be doers of the word, and not hearers only, deceiving your own selves. For if any man be a hearer of the word, and not a doer, he is like a man seeing his natural face in a glass. For he sees himself, and goes his way, and immediately forgets what manner of man he was. But whoever looks into the perfect law of liberty, and continues therein, he being not a forgetful hearer, but a doer of the work, this man shall be blessed in his deed. [James 1:22-25]

James points out that the man who hears the word only, but does not act upon or live by it, has deceived himself. For example, if

I had never been told that I was male, and all I had was a book of anatomy; and when I opened it, I saw that according to my parts, I was male—not female. However, if I, after seeing this truth, went about believing and telling people I was a woman, most people would think I was at least deceived. The same is true for the Christian who reads the Bible and sees that God says that in Christ he is righteous and holy, but then goes about believing and telling people he is nothing but an old sinner.

THE LORD OPENS THE EYES OF THE BLIND. THE LORD RAISES THEM THAT ARE BOWED DOWN. THE LORD LOVES THE RIGHTEOUS.

Psalm 146:8

James further likens this deceived person to a man who looks at his natural face in a mirror because all he can see is himself, and forgets what he had heard regarding the word of God. James then opens the door by which we can see the results of being both a hearer and a doer of the word. By looking into the "perfect law of liberty" or better said, the word of God (especially the New Testament) in which we see the image of the Lord, this person, if he continues to live according to what the word of God says, and not what the world says, and is not forgetful of what the word of God said, but rather he lives by the word, this man shall be blessed in his life. Most Christians, however, have trouble with being forgetful of what the Scripture says; and therefore, the devil can move you away from being confident in these truths.

The apostle Peter also wrote about these truths. In 2 Peter 1, he reminds us that we have been given *exceeding great and precious promises, that by these you might be partakers of the divine nature, having escaped the corruption that is in the world through lust.* [2 Peter 1:4]

Then he describes how by knowing that you have *escaped the corruption that is the world* (by being born again) you can use the truth of these promises to reveal the fruit of our salvation (see Galatians 5:22-23).

But for this very reason also, using therewith all diligence, in your faith have also virtue, in virtue knowledge, in knowledge temperance, in temperance endurance, in endurance godliness, in godliness brotherly love, in brotherly love love: for these things existing and abounding in you make [you] to be neither idle nor unfruitful as regards the knowledge of our Lord Jesus Christ; for he with whom these things are not present is blind, short-sighted, and has forgotten the purging of his former sins. Wherefore the rather, brethren, use diligence to make your calling and election sure, for doing these things you will never fall. [2 Peter 1:5-10 Darby Translation]

THEN BEWARE LEST YOU FORGET THE LORD, WHICH BROUGHT YOU FORTH OUT OF THE LAND OF EGYPT, FROM THE HOUSE OF BONDAGE.

Deut. 6:12

The apostle Peter is saying that by the promises of God, these things (faith, virtue, knowledge, temperance, patience, godliness, brotherly kindness, and love) exist in you and should be abounding in your life. And if you are lacking in these things, the word of God says that you are blind and have forgotten that you have been redeemed from your old sins (and sinful nature). This statement is particularly crucial to our understanding of spiritual truth and who we are in Christ.

The reason I chose to use the Darby Translation for this verse (as the King James substitutes the word "add" as in *add to your faith*) is because I believe the translation, at least in this verse, is more accurate and consistent with what Scripture teaches concerning what occurs when we are born again. Here's how I justified it: If we have received the faith (Ephesians 2:8), righteousness (Romans 5:17), peace (John 14:27), love (John 15:10), joy (John 15:11), and wisdom (1 Corinthians 1:30) of the Lord Jesus Christ, then it would not make sense that I would have to *add* any of these things to my faith. How much more do I need? Rather, I need to know that I already possess virtue, knowledge, temperance, endurance, godliness, brotherly kindness, and all the Fruit of the Spirit contained *in* my faith.

BEING NOW MADE FREE FROM SIN, AND BECOME SERVANTS TO GOD, YOU HAVE YOUR FRUIT UNTO HOLINESS, AND THE END EVERLAST-ING LIFE.

Romans 6:22

The fact that the fruit of the Spirit should be present and in abundance in a Christian's life isn't due to effort on their part, but rather it is a result or fruit of their salvation. Peter didn't say that if these are lacking in your life, then you should try to live a holier life. Instead, he said that you should remember that because you are born again, these things are present with you because of the indwelling of the Holy Spirit. Let's read the passage again, *for he with whom these things are not present is blind, short-sighted, and has forgotten the purging of his former sins.* What an awesome truth!

The fruit of the Spirit as stated in Galatians 5 (love, joy, peace, longsuffering, gentleness, goodness, faith, meekness, temperance) is not something we try to do. Making this claim would be like saying that an apple tree has to make an effort to produce apples. Fruit is a byproduct of a relationship, and the fruit of the Spirit is a byproduct, which happens naturally (or supernaturally) as a result of our relationship with Jesus Christ. As the Lord said in John 15:5: *I*

I AM WHAT I AM

am the vine; you are the branches. He that abides in me, and I in him, the same brings forth much fruit. For without me you can do nothing.

The final part of this series of verses from 2 Peter is perhaps the most crucial to realizing complete victory in Christ. *For if you do these things, you shall never fall.* [2 Peter 1:10] The realization that our identity and holiness has nothing to do with us, but everything to do with Jesus and His grace toward us can be the determining factor whether we hold fast the profession of our faith, or whether we fall from grace. Therefore, you don't become holier from the time you are born again to the time you leave your physical bodies. You are as holy as you will ever be (in the spirit) and by understanding that holiness is now part of your new nature, you will begin to have holiness manifest itself in greater measures in your physical life. For example, an apple tree doesn't bear much fruit in the beginning of its life, but as it grows, it bears more and more fruit as long as it remains rooted in the same ground. When it was young, it was still an apple tree—no different in makeup than any other apple tree. It didn't become a more apple-ly tree over the years—it simply produced more fruit as it grew.

The same is true with your life in Christ as the Lord said, *He who abides in me, and I in him, the same brings forth much fruit; for without me you can do nothing.* [John 15:5] The longer you remain rooted and grounded in what His word teaches concerning who you are, the more fruit you will bear; and this fruit is revealed in the life and character of Christ being manifested in your body.

THE FRUIT OF RIGHTEOUSNESS IS A TREE OF LIFE; AND HE THAT WINS SOULS IS WISE.

Proverbs 11:30

Being Made Blind So We Can See

To further support this teaching, let us turn back to the words of the Lord Jesus. In John 9:39-41, *Jesus said, For judgment I am come into this world, that they which see not might see; and they which see might be made blind. And some of the Pharisees which were with him heard these words, and said unto him, Are we blind also? Jesus said, If you were blind, you should have no sin. But now you say, We see. Therefore your sin remains.*

Here, the Lord is teaching us that He had come to open the eyes of those who have been blinded to spiritual truth (*they which see not might see*); and to blind them that perceive only the physical world (*they which see might be made blind*). We can get a better understanding of this passage when the Lord reiterates the same principle in John 12:37-40:

But though he had done so many miracles before them, yet they believed not on him. That the saying of Isaiah the prophet might be fulfilled, which he spoke, Lord, who has believed our report? And to whom has the arm of the Lord been revealed? Therefore they could not believe, because that Isaiah said again, He has blinded their eyes and hardened their heart; that they should not see with their eyes, nor understand with their heart, and be converted, and I should heal them.

The Lord's teaching of this principle can be found in Matthew, Mark, and Luke as well in response to the question why He spoke parables to the lost. Jesus said in Matthew 13:13, *Therefore I speak to*

I AM WHAT I AM

them in parables; because they seeing see not; and hearing they hear not, neither do they understand (see also Mark 4:12, Luke 8:10).

The importance of the passage earlier from John 9 is crucial in that when we are able to see spiritual truth as greater than physical truth, we should have no sin, which is the result of being born again. Remember the words of the Lord, *I am come into this world that they which see not might see; and they which see might be made blind.*

This principle is also taught in 2 Kings 6:15-17 when Gehazi, servant of the prophet Elisha, discovered early one morning that they were surrounded by the Syrian army. *And when the servant of the man of God was risen early, and gone forth, behold, a host compassed the city both with horses and chariots. And his servant said unto him, Alas, my master, how shall we do? And he answered, Fear not; for they that be with us are more than they that be with them. And Elisha prayed, and said, LORD, I pray, open his eyes, that he may see. And the LORD opened the eyes of the young man; and he saw; and behold, the mountain was full of horses and chariots of fire round about Elisha.*

This account teaches us the reality of spiritual truth as it relates to what we see in the natural. In the natural, Elisha and his servant were doomed. But (and fortunately) we are not dealing only with natural truths, but also with spiritual ones. What was true in the natural was trumped by what was true in the spirit, which, in this case, meant that the people of God would be victorious (as we can see through the rest of this passage from 2 Kings 6).

The great point this passage teaches is that the Scripture does

> NOW THEREFORE STAND AND SEE THIS GREAT THING, WHICH THE LORD WILL DO BEFORE YOUR EYES.
>
> *1 Samuel 12:16*

not say that as soon as Gehazi's eyes were opened the horses and chariots of fire arrived, indicating that they were already present. It was only when God opened his eyes did he perceive what was already present and true in the spirit, which is what I'm trying to teach here. And just to add more flavor to this, the Scripture never infers that Elisha ever actually saw what Gehazi did in the same way. I believe Elisha was operating completely by faith in God's word that promised *For he shall give his angels charge over you, to keep you in all your ways.* [Psalm 91:11] *The chariots of God are twenty thousand, even thousands of angels; the Lord is among them, as in Sinai, in the holy place.* [Psalm 68:17]

Therefore, since your eyes have been opened to the greater reality of who you are in the spirit realm, you should no longer view or see yourself as a sinner.

Because as he is, so are we in this world. [1 John 4:17]

WHO BEING THE BRIGHTNESS OF HIS GLORY, AND THE EXPRESS IMAGE OF HIS PERSON, AND UPHOLDING ALL THINGS BY THE WORD OF HIS POWER.

Hebrews 1:3

Scripture—A More Sure Foundation

For you have magnified your word above all your name. [Psalm 138:2]

Have you ever wondered why Jesus, the Word made flesh, quoted Scripture when He was confronted by Satan and tempted in the wilderness? Not only did He quote Scripture to Satan, but also during His teachings, He often referred back to what was already written in the law and the prophets. Why, when everything that came out of His mouth was Scripture, did Jesus use what was already written to support what He was saying? I mean,

I AM WHAT I AM

couldn't Jesus have improved on what had already been written? The answer is no, He couldn't.

As it relates to understanding your identity in Christ, the only reliable source is the written word of God. As the Lord Jesus is the humanly standard by which we should endeavor to imitate, the written word of God is what makes Jesus this standard. I want you to understand that I am in no way exalting the Bible above the person of God and the Lord Jesus. However, God has submitted Himself to His own word. He will not violate it because the entire universe is held together by its integrity (Hebrews 1:3).

Knowing this, you can be much more secure in what Scripture says concerning who you are in Christ. Again, I refer to what James wrote, *But whosoever looks into the perfect law of liberty, and continues therein, he being not a forgetful hearer, but a doer of the work, this man shall be blessed in his deed.* [James 1:25] The perfect law of liberty James is referring to is the written word of God, which includes what God meant to eventually be part of the New Testament Scriptures.

So many in the body of Christ have been searching for truth through an emotional high, or a physical touch from God—one that makes you collapse in joy, or a word from the pastor or a prophet. They relate all spiritual truth by the number of goose bumps or tingling sensations they feel, or if it makes people jump, dance, shout, or run around a building. Many see that if the preacher isn't wearing a $1,000 suit and isn't wiping his fevered brow, dancing and gyrating, and speaking in shifting tones and pace, he isn't "under

SO SHALL MY WORD BE THAT GOES OUT OF MY MOUTH. IT SHALL NOT RETURN UNTO ME VOID, BUT IT SHALL ACCOMPLISH THAT WHICH I PLEASE, AND IT SHALL PROSPER IN THE THING WHERETO I SENT IT.

Isaiah 55:11

the anointing." Everything is measured by what they feel, hear, and see instead of what it really should, which is the written word of God.

I once said, "I wish I could have walked with Jesus when He was here on earth." I've heard many people say the same or similar thing, thinking that their relationship with God would be better if they could have been with the physical Jesus. I've also said, "I wish God would speak to me in an audible voice, so I can hear Him better." I'm sure you or someone you know has said the very same thing.

SPEAK THE WORD ONLY AND MY SERVANT SHALL BE HEALED.

Matthew 8:8

You know, actually walking with the Lord during His ministry, and hearing the audible voice of God are exciting to think about, but they are not equal to knowing and hearing God through His written word. In fact, the Lord Jesus said, *Nevertheless I tell you the truth. It is expedient for you that I go away. For if I go not away, the Comforter will not come unto you. But if I depart, I will send him unto you.* [John 16:7]

Jesus said it was <u>better for us</u> for Him to go away so we could know Him through the Spirit rather than the flesh. God prefers that you relate to Him through faith and in the spirit rather than through physical things.

The apostle Peter wrote it this way, *For we have not followed cunningly devised fables, when we made known unto you the power and coming of our Lord Jesus Christ, but were witnesses of his majesty. For he received from God the Father honor and glory, when there came such a voice to him from the excellent glory, This is my beloved Son, in whom I*

I AM WHAT I AM

am well pleased. And this voice which came from heaven we heard, when we were with him in the holy mount. We have also a more sure word of prophecy; whereunto you do well that you take heed, as unto a light that shines in a dark place, until the day dawns, and the day star arises in your hearts. Knowing this first, that no prophecy of the scripture is of any private interpretation. For the prophecy came not in old time by the will of man; but holy men of God spoke as they were moved by the Holy Ghost. [2 Peter 1:16-21]

When he wrote this second epistle, Peter was approaching the end of his life and this letter was the means by which he could stir up the readers by putting them in remembrance of what he had previously taught (2 Peter 1:13). He first appeals to their reasoning, that they had not followed some mythical ghost, but were eyewitnesses to what the Lord Jesus both taught and did. In fact, Peter cites hearing the voice of God when He said about Jesus, *This is my beloved Son in whom I am well pleased.* However, in spite of what they heard and saw with their physical eyes and ears, Peter returns to the more sure word of prophecy that is contained in the Scriptures to verify the truth of the Lord Jesus.

Peter cautions the reader to consider carefully what he is about to read, as the written word of God is like the light that shines in a dark place; and by knowing this first—that is, using the written word of God as the primary source of revelation and truth—that no prophecy can be interpreted in a way that violates the harmony of Scripture, even if the person says, "Thus saith the Lord."

AND THAT FROM A CHILD YOU HAVE KNOWN THE HOLY SCRIP-TURES, WHICH ARE ABLE TO MAKE YOU WISE UNTO SALVATION THROUGH FAITH WHICH IS IN CHRIST JESUS.

2 Timothy 3:15

Then, beginning in chapter 2, Peter begins his warnings about false prophets and teachers, bringing in damnable heresies, even denying the Lord, and with false words they will make merchandise of the people. We see this so much in the Christian world today through some television ministries, and crusades where false prophets come to town and spoil the already financially-struggling people into "sowing a seed" in order for God to bless them.

We see this principle also in John 2:18-22 when Jesus prophesied about His death and resurrection. *Then answered the Jews and said unto him, What sign do you show to us, seeing that you do these things? Jesus answered and said unto them, Destroy this temple, and in three days I will raise it up. Then the Jews said, Forty-six years was this temple in building, and you will rear it up in three days? But he spoke of the temple of his body. When therefore he was risen from the dead, his disciples remembered that he had said this to them; and they believed the scripture, and the word which Jesus had said.*

The disciples, although hearing the physical voice of Jesus predicting His own death and resurrection, first believed the Scripture and then the word Jesus had spoken. This passage supports that the written word of God is the acid test to everything you read and hear. Even though I am very confident that this book is in harmony with what Scripture teaches, I am not above being deceived or making a mistake, which is why you should be verifying everything contained in this book by what is written in the Bible.

It is the written word of God that is the more sure foundation as

I AM WHAT I AM

it is written, *All scripture is given by inspiration of God, and is profitable for doctrine, for reproof, for correction, for instruction in righteousness, that the man of God may be perfect, thoroughly furnished unto all good works.* [2 Timothy 3:16-17]

PROVE ALL THINGS; HOLD FAST THAT WHICH IS GOOD.

1 Thess. 5:21

But against any of the children of Israel shall not a dog move his tongue, against man or beast; that you may know how the LORD does put a difference between the Egyptians and Israel.

EXODUS 11:7

PART IV

Who You Are in Christ

And I myself also am persuaded of you, my brethren, that you also are full of goodness, filled with all knowledge, able also to admonish one another.

ROMANS 15:14

Blessed is the man that trusts in the LORD, and whose hope the LORD is. For he shall be as a tree planted by the waters, and that spreads out her roots by the river, and shall not see when heat comes, but her leaf shall be green; and shall not be careful in the year of drought, neither shall cease from yielding fruit.

JEREMIAH 17:7-8

11

Righteousness

Being filled with the fruits of righteousness, which are by Christ Jesus, unto the glory and praise of God.

PHILIPPIANS 1:11

IN HIS DAYS JUDAH SHALL BE SAVED, AND ISRAEL SHALL DWELL SAFELY; AND THIS IS HIS NAME WHEREBY HE SHALL BE CALLED, THE LORD OUR RIGHTEOUS-NESS.

Jeremiah 23:6

In Christ you are righteous. Along with many other terms, righteous and righteousness have become religious clichés that have lost their meaning to many people. Many Christians are unsure of what righteousness is, preventing them from understanding what it takes to have a relationship with God.

"Righteousness" and "righteous," appear 542 times in 512 verses of the Bible. In contrast, "faith," "faithfulness" and "faithful" are only used 348 times in 328 verses. This means that there are 1.5 times as many scriptures about righteousness as there are about faith. Therefore, we can rightly conclude that righteousness is important.

So what does righteousness mean? Righteousness is the condition of being in *right* standing or relationship with God. This can only happen through total faith and dependence upon Christ, as the Bible says, *For by grace are you saved through faith; and that not of yourselves; it is the gift of God.* [Ephesians 2:8] There is no other way to be righteous and there is nothing we can do on our own to accomplish this. It's either all grace or all works and not a combination of the two. To quote Bible teacher Andrew Wommack, "Jesus plus something equals nothing; but Jesus plus nothing equals everything." He was simply summarizing what the apostle Paul wrote in Romans 11:6, *And if by grace, then it is no more of works; otherwise grace is no more grace. But if it be of works, then it is no more grace; otherwise work is no more work.*

Furthermore, righteousness is not a character trait of a Christian; but rather the Christian bears fruit of his or her right standing and relationship with God, which we call works of righteousness. This truth is vital when seeking to fully understand righteousness and how we receive it and walk in it.

The Righteousness of God

But now the righteousness of God without the law is manifested, being witnessed by the law and the prophets. Even the righteousness of God, which is by faith of Jesus Christ unto all and upon all them that believe; for there is no difference. [Romans 3:21-22]

The Lord Jesus and His righteousness is the standard by which everyone is measured by God in order to have relationship with Him. Jesus was completely sinless, pure, and holy, and therefore was able to not only have relationship with the Father, but to be in union with Him. For us, the Bible teaches that all of us *have sinned and come*

EVERY WORD OF GOD IS PURE; HE IS A SHIELD UNTO THEM THAT PUT THEIR TRUST IN HIM.

Proverbs 30:5

I AM WHAT I AM

short of the glory of God [Romans 3:23] and that *all our righteousnesses are as filthy rags.* [Isaiah 64:6] Therefore, how can anyone other than Jesus have relationship with God? The answer is that no one can if he is trusting in his own righteousness. We must have a righteousness that exceeds anything we could ever produce through our own effort. This is where Jesus comes in. He has made the way for us to not only have relationship with God, but to be in union with God as well through the Spirit.

Many Christian and biblical scholars view the Lord's "Sermon on the Mount" (Matthew 5-7) as an instruction in righteousness and way of life. While definitely a teaching on righteousness, I would disagree that the sermon—specifically chapter 5—was a "How-To" for living a godly life. After what are called the beatitudes (Matthew 5:3-16) the Lord begins to make reference to the law and the prophets (or the Old Testament).

Think not that I am come to destroy the law, or the prophets; I am not come to destroy, but to fulfill. For truly I say unto you, Till heaven and earth pass, one jot or one tittle shall in no wise pass from the law, till all be fulfilled. [Matthew 5:17-18]

The Bible teaches that the law was given to Moses, not as a set of rules by which we should aspire to live, but rather, to show us the exceedingly high standard God requires in order to be in relationship with Him, and how much we need a savior to be restored. Many people, including Christians, view the law, especially the Ten Commandments, as the basis for the way we should live. While I agree

PROVE ALL THINGS; HOLD FAST THAT WHICH IS GOOD.

1 Thess. 5:21

(as the apostle Paul agreed) that the law was perfect, and that in it, had a display of wisdom (Colossians 2:20-23), it is humanly impossible for anyone (other than Jesus) to keep all of it. And this is what Jesus intended to teach us in this message.

Immediately after the beatitudes, the Lord Jesus said, *For I say unto you, That except your righteousness shall exceed the righteousness of the scribes and Pharisees, you shall in no case enter into the kingdom of heaven.* [Matthew 5:20]

When one is able to understand the comparison the Lord is making (to the Pharisees and scribes) we can see that whoever heard His words was shocked because the Pharisees and scribes were viewed as the holiest people in Israel. They made long prayers, fasted twice a week, and paid tithes of mint, anise, and cumin. If their righteousness had to exceed that of the scribes and Pharisees, they had to conclude it was impossible to enter into the kingdom of heaven. And this is what the Lord was teaching—that it was impossible for anyone to enter into the kingdom of God in their own righteousness.

After this statement, the Lord begins going through the commandments beginning with murder. With each commandment, Jesus reveals a more strict application to it, thereby conveying the impossibility of keeping the law in our own strength. Not only could you not murder, but if you were angry with someone without cause you would be guilty of the same offense. In the sense of sexual sin, not only could you not commit adultery, but if you looked upon a

I AM WHAT I AM

woman (or man) with lust, you were guilty of the same offense. I'm sure there were people there who like the rich young ruler in Matthew 19:16, believed they had kept all the commandments. They hadn't murdered anyone; nor had they committed adultery, stolen, or even told a lie. However, the Lord was leveling the playing field, inferring as the Scripture concludes that all men are under sin, so He could have mercy upon us all (Galatians 3:21-22).

The Lord used the commandments as they were intended, which as it is written in Galatians 3:24-26 to be *our schoolmaster to bring us to Christ, that we might be justified by faith. But after that faith is come, we are no longer under a schoolmaster. For you are all the children of God by faith in Jesus Christ.*

Therefore, once we are in Christ, we are no longer in need of the law. Paul wrote in 1 Timothy 1:8-11 that *the law is good, if a man uses it lawfully. Knowing this, that the law is not made for the righteous man, but for the lawless and disobedient, for the ungodly and sinners, for unholy and profane, for murderers of fathers, and murderers of mothers, for manslayers, for whoremongers, for them that defile themselves with mankind, for menstealers, for liars, for perjured persons, and if there be any other thing that is contrary to sound doctrine, according to the glorious gospel of the blessed God, which was committed to my trust.*

Therefore, as the Lord Jesus proclaimed, He did not come to nullify or destroy the law because God's standards cannot be changed. God's divine justice had to be served, and since no person born under the curse of sin could be righteous enough for God, and because

IF YOU KNOW THAT HE IS RIGHTEOUS, YOU KNOW THAT EVERY ONE THAT DOES RIGHTEOUS-NESS IS BORN OF HIM.

I John 2:29

of God's great love for us, He sent His only begotten Son to the world to suffer the wrath and judgment of God for us so that He could reconcile His beloved creation to Himself. Because Jesus fulfilled the requirements of God's law, His righteousness is imparted unto us through faith.

This is what Jesus meant in Matthew 6:33 when He said, *But seek first the kingdom of God, and His righteousness and all these things shall be added unto you.* Many people view this passage to mean that we should seek the kingdom of God and also seek His righteousness, and then all the things He mentioned (clothing, provision, etc.) will be added unto us. While I agree that we should definitely seek to walk in God's righteousness, I submit that the Lord was really telling us that if we seek the kingdom of God through placing our complete trust in the sacrifice of Jesus Christ, then His righteousness and all these other things would be added unto us.

The Gift of Righteousness

Perhaps the greatest hindrance to having full comprehension of righteousness is the misunderstanding of how we become righteous in God's eyes. It is commonly believed that our righteousness is determined by our actions. While there is a link between our actions and our right standing with God, our relationship with God produces actions or fruit, not the other way around. In other words, we do not become righteous by what we do, but because we are righteous, we bear the fruit of righteousness.

I AM WHAT I AM

The Bible teaches that righteousness is a gift from God and is imparted to those who accept and rely on what Jesus has done for them to reconcile them to God. Therefore, by grace, we receive the righteousness of Jesus that makes us "right" with God. *For if by one man's offense death reigned by one, much more they which receive abundance of grace and the gift of righteousness shall reign in life by one Jesus Christ.* [Romans 5:17]

When a person is born again, his heart is changed, which results in a change of behavior, or fruit of righteousness. Unfortunately, many in the church have been taught that actions and prohibitions are what bring change in a person. This deception has resulted in the growth of Christian activism where Christians are focusing their efforts on legislating and protesting instead of preaching the gospel, which is the power of God unto salvation. Someone was quoted, "Julius Caesar tried to change men by changing the world; but Jesus Christ changed the world by changing men."

And this is exactly what Jesus taught in Matthew 23:25-26, when the Lord chastised the Pharisees and scribes saying, *Woe unto you, scribes and Pharisees, hypocrites! For you make clean the outside of the cup and of the platter, but within they are full of extortion and excess. You blind Pharisees, cleanse first that which is within the cup and platter, that the outside of them may be clean also.* The Lord is teaching that only through a changed heart will you see true fruit of righteousness.

The apostle Paul described the manifestation of God's righteous-

> I PUT ON RIGHTEOUSNESS AND IT CLOTHED ME; MY JUDGMENT WAS AS A ROBE AND A DIADEM.
>
> *Job 29:14*

ness in us and called it the Fruit of the Spirit (Galatians 5:22-23). Paul also confirmed this truth in Philippians 3:9 *And be found in him, not having mine own righteousness, which is of the law, but that which is through the faith of Christ, the righteousness which is of God by faith.*

Declared Righteous

THEY SHALL COME AND DECLARE HIS RIGH-TEOUSNESS UNTO A PEOPLE THAT SHALL BE BORN, THAT HE HAS DONE THIS.

Psalm 22:31

To declare, I say, at this time his righteousness that he might be just, and the justifier of him who believes in Jesus. [Romans 3:26]

Because Jesus completely fulfilled the righteousness of the law, God has declared all who will trust in Jesus righteous in His sight. The Bible says that Jesus *condemned sin in the flesh, that the righteousness of the law might be fulfilled in us.* [Romans 8:3-4] This is an awesome truth—that God, because of Jesus, has called us righteous as long as we rely on the righteousness of Jesus alone—and not our own righteousness. Again, this is where the devil has deceived many in the church—that God deals with us according to our own righteousness and performance instead of the righteousness of the Lord Jesus. Most Christians fully accept that it is Jesus alone who is responsible for their initial salvation, but many unfortunately fall into the same trap the church of Galatia had fallen into where they had turned back to the weak and beggarly elements of following the law to keep them saved. The apostle Paul asked, *Are you so foolish— having begun in the Spirit, are you now made perfect by the flesh?* [Galatians 3:3]

As God called Abram the father of many nations when he had

I AM WHAT I AM

no children, God was illustrating what He would eventually do for us by declaring us righteous by faith.

A great illustration of this truth is found through the bald eagle. In 1782, the 2nd Continental Congress officially declared the bald eagle the National Emblem of the United States. Most students of U.S. history will remember the controversy surrounding the choice of the eagle as the country's emblem. History teaches us that Benjamin Franklin strongly opposed using the bald eagle saying, "For my part, I wish the eagle had not been chosen as the representative of this county. He is a bird of bad moral character; he does not get his living honestly. You may have seen him perched in some dead tree where, too lazy to fish for himself, he watches the labor of the fishing hawk and, when that diligent bird has at length taken a fish and is bearing it to his nest for his young ones, the bald eagle pursues him and takes the fish. With all this injustice, he is never in good case."

While the eagle, in all appearances is a majestic bird representing honor and courage, it is actually, by nature, a glorified buzzard, feeding himself by the labor of others, or from roadkill. However, by no merit of its own, the bald eagle has been declared majestic, and is viewed to be honorable, and a symbol of the greatest and most courageous nation ever to exist on the face of this earth.

By the same token, because of the Lord Jesus, we, who were by nature children of wrath, have been declared righteous by God by no merit of our own. Furthermore, while viewed as an honorable

FOR THOUGH YOUR PEOPLE ISRAEL ARE AS THE SAND IN THE SEA; YET A REMNANT OF THEM SHALL RETURN. THE CONSUMP-TION DECREED SHALL OVERFLOW WITH RIGHTEOUS-NESS.

Isaiah 10:22

and majestic symbol of a great nation, the inherent nature of the eagle has not changed: it continues to behave as Benjamin Franklin illustrated "he is never in good case."

Fortunately for us, we have a better case than the bald eagle—in that not only are we declared righteous by God, but we are actually made righteous.

Made Righteous

For he has made him to be sin for us, who knew no sin, that we might be made the righteousness of God in him. [2 Corinthians 5:21]

That we have been declared righteous by God when we place faith in the righteousness of Jesus Christ is a glorious truth, but this is not the extent of God's grace. In Christ we have much more. While the Old Testament saints like Abraham and David were declared righteous by faith, we, under the New Testament in Jesus Christ, have a much better state. In addition to being declared righteous by God, we are *made* righteous by the grace of God through the power of the Holy Spirit. This is the essence of the new creature as described in 2 Corinthians 5:17: *Therefore if any man be in Christ, he is a new creature. Old things are passed away; behold, all things are become new.*

Once we are born again, our nature changes from that of the devil to the nature of God. This "new man" is what the Lord described to Nicodemus in John 3; and it has been created righteous. The Bible teaches us to *put on the new man, which after God is created in righteousness and true holiness.* [Ephesians 4:24]

I used the example of the eagle in the previous section to illustrate how we are declared righteous by God; but now I will use a caterpillar to illustrate how we are made righteous by God.

Most people are familiar with the term metamorphosis, the process by which a caterpillar is changed or transformed into a butterfly. This same word in the Greek *metamorphoo* is used only four times in the New Testament and was translated "transfigured", "transformed" and "changed". Transformation and change refers to what occurs when we are born again; and the other transfigured refers to the Lord Jesus when He was transfigured (Matthew 17).

Be not conformed to this world, but be <u>transformed</u> *by the renewing of your mind, that you may prove what is that good, and acceptable, and perfect will of God.* [Romans 12:2]

But we all with open face beholding as in a glass the glory of the Lord, are <u>changed</u> *into the same image from glory to glory, even as by the Spirit of the Lord.* [2 Corinthians 3:18]

The comparison of what occurs when we are born again and the metamorphosis of the caterpillar is compelling. The short life of a caterpillar is spent crawling on the ground, consuming everything in its path, not producing anything of real value to the world, other than food for predators. Similarly, according to Scripture, our existence apart from Christ is spent much the same way—living by the lusts of our flesh, seeking only what contributes to the fulfillment of self, being ripe prey for an enemy who has blinded us to the truth of

AWAKE TO RIGHTEOUS-NESS AND SIN NOT. FOR SOME HAVE NOT THE KNOWL-EDGE OF GOD. I SPEAK THIS TO YOUR SHAME.

1 Cor. 15:34

not only his existence, but of the knowledge and glory of God. The Bible says that we *were dead in trespasses and sins; wherein in time past you walked according to the course of this world, according to the prince of the power of the air, the spirit that now works in the children of disobedience; among whom also we all had our conversation in times past in the lusts of our flesh, fulfilling the desires of the mind; and were by nature the children of wrath, even as others.* [Ephesians 2:1-3]

But, if it's not consumed by a predator before, the caterpillar is led instinctively to spin a cocoon and wrap itself within its changing power, emerging a completely transformed being. When as a caterpillar, it spent its life crawling and consuming, now the new butterfly spends its life flying and giving life and peace to the world. How great a contrast of the two natures!

For us, we have a similar transformation. Whereas before when we were by nature servants of the devil, God has provided the gospel by which we are led to the loving arms and heart of God, a cocoon of redemption from which we truly never emerge, being sealed by the Spirit of God whereby we can walk as a completely new creature. And as the butterfly, the new creature in Christ now gives life (salt and light) to the world.

But God, who is rich in mercy, for his great love wherewith he loved us, has quickened (made us alive) *us together with Christ (by grace you are saved) and has raised us up together, and made us sit together in heavenly places in Christ Jesus; that in the ages to come he might show the exceeding riches of his grace in his kindness toward us through Christ*

I WILL BEAR THE INDIGNA-
TION OF THE LORD, BECAUSE I HAVE SINNED AGAINST HIM, UNTIL HE PLEAD MY CAUSE AND EXECUTE JUDGMENT FOR ME. HE WILL BRING ME FORTH TO THE LIGHT, AND I WILL BEHOLD HIS RIGHTEOUS-
NESS.

Micah 7:9

I AM WHAT I AM

Jesus. For by grace are you saved through faith; and that not of your-selves. It is the gift of God; not of works, lest any man should boast. For we are his workmanship, created in Christ Jesus unto good works, which God has before ordained that we should walk in them. [Ephesians 2:4-10]

But of him are you in Christ Jesus, who of God is made unto us wis-dom, and righteousness, and sanctification, and redemption, *that, ac-cording as it is written, He that glories, let him glory in the Lord.* [1 Corinthians 1:30-31]

Again, as with the eagle, we see the transformation of a caterpil-lar to a butterfly as glorious. However, in Christ, our transformation is much more glorious. We are of more value than many sparrows, as the Lord said in Matthew 10:31. While the butterfly has gone through such a dramatic transformation, the truth is that this trans-formation is more like a child becoming an adult than what occurs when we are born again. The caterpillar is but one stage of the life of a butterfly—the larvae stage; and although it acts in a different man-ner, it is not a different species of being. The Bible says *Therefore if any man be in Christ, he is a new creature. Old things are passed away; behold, all things are become new; and all things are of God who has reconciled us to himself by Jesus Christ, and has given to us the ministry of reconciliation.* [2 Corinthians 5:17-18]

Therefore, according to Scripture, any person in Christ is a com-pletely new creature—different from the person he was before. Simi-lar to the butterfly, when we are born again, we are given a new nature, meaning that we have been changed from the inside, which

FOR AS BY ONE MAN'S DISOBEDI-ENCE MANY WERE MADE SINNERS, SO BY THE OBEDIENCE OF ONE SHALL MANY BE MADE RIGHTEOUS.

Romans 5:19

will produce outward expressions or fruit of this change. Because of our new nature, we should not desire to live the same life we lived before this transformation. While your old sinful nature lived according to the ways of the world, your new nature desires to live according the word of God. After emerging from the cocoon, the butterfly doesn't desire to crawl on the ground anymore; neither does it proclaim to be only a glorified caterpillar, or a worm transformed by cocoon. The truth is that the caterpillar, by its own actions, reveals an understanding of it being dead to being a caterpillar and alive to being a butterfly. And this is what we must do, but unfortunately, most Christian churches do not teach and embrace the truths of the Bible that teach that in Christ we are dead to sin and have been given a new nature. Instead, they still see themselves as sinners, and use the term "sinner saved by grace."

This is what the apostle Paul was teaching in Romans 6:2-14 when the question of continuing to live in sin when grace would abound. *How shall we who are dead to sin live any longer therein? Do you not know that so many of us as were baptized into Jesus Christ were baptized into his death? Therefore we are buried with him by baptism into death, that like as Christ was raised up from the dead by the glory of the Father, even so we also should walk in the newness of life. For if we have been planted together in the likeness of his death, we shall be also in the likeness of his resurrection. Knowing this, that our old man* (nature) *is crucified with him, that the body of sin might be destroyed, that henceforth we should not serve sin. For he that is dead is freed from sin.*

FOR THEY BEING IGNORANT OF GOD'S RIGHTEOUSNESS, AND GOING ABOUT TO ESTABLISH THEIR OWN RIGHTEOUSNESS, HAVE NOT SUBMITTED THEMSELVES UNTO THE RIGHTEOUSNESS OF GOD.

Romans 10:3

I AM WHAT I AM

Now if we are dead with Christ, we believe that we shall also live with him. Knowing that Christ being raised from the dead can die no more; death has no more dominion over him. For in that he died, he died unto sin once; but in that he lives, he lives unto God. Likewise reckon yourselves to be dead indeed to sin (once as Christ did), *and alive unto God through Jesus Christ our Lord. Let not sin therefore reign in your mortal body, that you should obey it in the lusts thereof. Neither yield your members as instruments of unrighteousness unto sin; but yield yourselves unto God, as those who are alive from the dead, and your members as instruments of righteousness unto God. For sin shall not have dominion over you; for you are not under the law, but under grace.*

SUBMIT YOURSELVES THEREFORE UNTO GOD. RESIST THE DEVIL AND HE WILL FLEE FROM YOU.

James 4:7

What a powerful teaching this is! Because of our new nature in Christ, we, being dead to sin, are no longer compelled to live in sin, but to live for God. Grace has broken the power of sin over our lives, and by grace we should not desire to live in sin. Why? Because we are dead to sin and our nature has changed.

Unfortunately, many Christians have neither understood nor embraced the truth of the new creature. Therefore, their view of their new identity in Christ is similar to a pig. You can take a pig out of the sty, give it a bath, dress it up and put perfume and makeup on it, and it will look pretty for a while, but sooner or later, it will break free from your control and head right back into the sty and wallow in the mud. Why does it do this? Because it's the pig's nature to wallow in the mud. A pig's nature does not change, but ours does. Praise God!

Unlike the pig, eagle, or caterpillar who don't have a choice to change, people do have a choice to allow God to change them through the gospel.

To further support the truth of the new creature, we are also given a new name. Our identity is contained in a name. Adam named all the animals and even though they existed without a name, they had no identity. The Latin name that identifies both the caterpillar and butterfly does not change throughout its existence, but ours does. As a bride takes the name of her husband, we take the name of Christ when we are born again. When before we were sinners; now we are Christians. In Revelation 2:17 and 3:12, the Lord said He was going to give those who overcome a new name—His new name (see also Isaiah 62:2).

AND THE GENTILES SHALL SEE YOUR RIGHTEOUSNESS, AND ALL KINGS YOUR GLORY; AND YOU SHALL BE CALLED BY A NEW NAME, WHICH THE MOUTH OF THE LORD SHALL NAME.

Isaiah 62:2

Holiness

And that you put on the new man, which after God is created in righteousness and true holiness.

EPHESIANS 4:24

In the same way that righteousness has been misinterpreted by many Christians, holiness has as well. If you were to poll most people—even non-Christians—and ask them to define holiness, most would describe it as a behavior, way of living, or character trait. However, while man tends to look only at the outward appearance, not considering the root cause, God looks at the root or the heart of things.

As I mentioned before, holiness is a fruit or byproduct of our relationship or right standing with God. Therefore, the definition of holiness as a manifestation of good works and behavior is correct. What we must first understand about holiness is that since it is fruit, it can only be born from a seed; and since a seed only produces fruit after its own kind, we cannot bear fruit of holiness without the seed of holiness having been planted in us. And this is where any teaching on holiness must begin—with the seed.

The seed that produces holiness is the righteousness of God that is imparted unto us by faith upon being born again and receiving the Spirit of God. Since we are new creatures in Christ Jesus, and created by God in righteousness and true holiness, we should be bearing fruit of this righteousness in the form of a holy lifestyle.

Many Christians have been taught that we should live a holy life to please God, so that He will bless our lives. This way of thinking is legalism; and truthfully, it is an offense to God, because when a person comes to God on his own merit, and not by faith in the merit of Jesus Christ, they are nullifying the grace of God, and depreciating the value of the death of the Lord Jesus (Galatians 2:21; Galatians 5:4).

The Bible says, *But without faith it is impossible to please him* [Hebrews 11:6] and *So then they that are in the flesh cannot please God.* [Romans 8:8]

Some people have taken the following passage of Scripture to support living a holy life in order to please and receive from God. *Follow peace with all men, and holiness, without which no man shall see the Lord.* [Hebrews 12:14] Because all of us have been conditioned that we are rewarded or penalized based on our performance, this passage fits perfectly into a theology that is based on works. If we strive to live according to all of God's commands and laws, then we will be able to see and please the Lord. Consequently, our holy lives will be rewarded with blessings of health, financial prosperity, etc.

I've also seen this passage quoted in the same context, *And whatsoever we ask, we receive of him, because we keep his commandments,*

BE THEREFORE PERFECT, EVEN AS YOUR FATHER WHICH IS IN HEAVEN IS PERFECT.

Matthew 5:48

I AM WHAT I AM

and do those things that are pleasing in his sight. [1 John 3:22] This verse was used in a devotional teaching on obedience, saying that God's answers to our prayers are based on whether we keep His commandments, and do those things that are pleasing in His sight. I was shocked and disappointed, because this tells me that the writer has no concept of God's grace.

This mindset is exactly what the apostle Paul tried to correct in his letter to the Galatians. While having been born again after hearing the gospel, legalistic Christians had corrupted them with a perversion of the gospel that Paul had preached, causing them to be in bondage to the law of works and circumcision. Although the letter of Hebrews and 1 John had not been written at the time of Paul's letter to the Galatians, we can assume that the legalistic Christians used similar language in their teachings.

When anyone cites these passages of Scripture as a basis for living a holy life in order to please God and get their prayers answered, I always have them continue to subsequent verses in order to clarify what the writer is actually saying. In both letters (Hebrews and 1 John) the point of faith is made explicitly clear. The apostle John elaborates what it means to *keep His commandments* as it is written, *And this is his commandment, That we should believe on the name of his Son Jesus Christ, and love one another as he gave us commandment. And he that keeps his commandments dwells in him, and he in him. And hereby we know that he abides in us, by the Spirit which he has given us.* [1 John 3:23-24]

JESUS ANSWERED AND SAID UNTO THEM. THIS IS THE WORK OF GOD, THAT YOU BELIEVE ON HIM WHOM HE HAS SENT.

John 6:29

In Paul's letter to the Hebrews, he clarifies that what he wrote in verse 14 refers to Whom we should be following—not *what* we should be following: *Looking diligently lest any man fail of the grace of God...* [Hebrews 12:15]

He is simply repeating himself from what he wrote in verse 2 of this chapter, *Looking unto Jesus, the author and finisher of our faith; who for the joy that was set before him endured the cross, despising the shame, and is set down at the right hand of the throne of God.*

It is easy to see that Paul is not talking about performance, but about receiving grace through faith. The only way we can fail the grace of God is by failing to trust in the righteousness of the Lord Jesus as being the only way of having relationship with God. If you are trusting in your own righteousness, which is according to your obedience to the law, then you are frustrating the grace of God as it is written, *I do not frustrate the grace of God; for if righteousness comes by the law, then Christ is dead in vain.* [Galatians 2:21]

Furthermore, when the passage from Hebrews 12:14 instructs the Christian to *follow peace with all men, and holiness, without which no man shall see the Lord*, this refers to how we should be reflecting the character of Christ in our lives. In other words, we should follow peace and holiness, without which no man shall see the Lord *in us*.

Holiness is not something accomplished from our own efforts. Rather, it should come naturally, and without effort, because it is the nature of God to produce holy fruit. And since we are in Christ, we have the nature of God, and have been created in righteousness and

I AM WHAT I AM

true holiness, holy fruit should be produced effortlessly.

In the natural realm, we can look at an apple tree and see that it does not struggle and travail to produce apples. You don't hear wood cracking and growing pains just before the apple blossoms—it happens naturally because it's the apple tree's nature.

Although this is simply said, it not easily accomplished. The reason is for the most part, the Christian church has taught that holiness is a result of discipline and keeping of God's law, instead of allowing the word of God to change the way you think and see yourself in Christ. This transformation occurs through renewing of your mind, and through the realization of who you are in Christ—having been created in righteousness and true holiness.

AND IF CHRIST BE IN YOU, THE BODY IS DEAD BECAUSE OF SIN; BUT THE SPIRIT IS LIFE BECAUSE OF RIGHTEOUSNESS.

Romans 8:10

13

Sanctification

> *But of him are you in Christ Jesus, who of God is made unto us wisdom, righteousness, and sanctification, and redemption.*
>
> 1 CORINTHIANS 1: 30

WHO GAVE HIMSELF FOR US, THAT HE MIGHT REDEEM US FROM ALL INIQUITY, AND PURIFY UNTO HIMSELF A PECULIAR PEOPLE, ZEALOUS OF GOOD WORKS.

Titus 2:14

As with righteousness and holiness, sanctification is a fruit or byproduct of your relationship with the Lord. According to the Bible to be sanctified means to be made holy, purify, or consecrated. In fact, the Greek word *hagiazo* is used interchangeably when referring sanctification and holiness. As Christians we are sanctified by God when we are born again, and like righteousness and holiness, we are to bear fruit of this fact in our lives.

The sanctification that most Christians are familiar with is the process of living a life separated from the influence of the world. In this sense sanctification means to be set apart for service unto God. Because you have been sanctified by God, your sanctification is a done deal, similar to being sealed by the Holy Spirit until the day of redemption. The Bible says, *By the which will* (referring to the new covenant in Christ) *we are sanctified through the offering of Jesus Christ*

I AM WHAT I AM

once and for all. For by one offering he has perfected forever them that are sanctified. [Hebrews 10:10, 14]

Therefore, as with holiness, the fact you are living a holy life, separated from all the corruption in the world, not partaking in its desires and lusts, simply means that you are bearing fruit of what God has already accomplished in you.

The most prominent teaching about living separate from the world was written by the apostle Paul in 2 Corinthians 6:14-7:1:

Be not unequally yoked together with unbelievers. For what fellowship does righteousness have with unrighteousness? And what communion does light have with darkness? And what concord does Christ have with Belial? Or what part does he that believes have with an infidel? And what agreement does the temple of God have with idols? For you are the temple of the living God as God has said, I will dwell in them; and I will be their God, and they shall be my people. Wherefore come out from among them, and be separate, says the Lord, and touch not the unclean thing; and I will receive you. And will be a Father unto you, and you shall be my sons and daughters, says the Lord Almighty. Having therefore these promises, dearly beloved, let us cleanse ourselves from all filthiness of the flesh and spirit, perfecting holiness in the fear of God.

The Lord desires that you walk in sanctification the same as you walk in holiness; and for the same reasons—because He loves you and wants only the best for His children. The Bible teaches that the things of the world will corrupt you as it is written, *Be not deceived; evil communications corrupt good manners.* [1 Corinthians 15:33] The

THAT EVERY ONE OF YOU SHOULD KNOW HOW TO POSSESS HIS VESSEL IN SANCTIFICATION AND HONOR.

1 Thess. 4:4

Amplified Bible translates this verse as, *Evil companionships (communion, associations) corrupt and deprave good manners, and morals, and character.*

So, knowing that God desires for us to avoid evil associations and relationships, how do we endeavor to keep ourselves separate from them. First of all, a truly born again Christian is going to experience at least some degree of change in their heart toward some or most of the things they used to do. However, the Bible teaches that this is not always the case, and consequently we have these scriptures to learn from.

The last passage from Paul's teaching in 2 Corinthians gives us a glimpse of how we accomplish walking in our sanctification. He first reminds us of who we are in Christ and the promises God made, which he cited in the previous verses. *For <u>you are the temple of the living God</u> as God has said, I will dwell in them; and I will be their God, and <u>they shall be my people</u>. Wherefore come out from among them, and be separate, says the Lord, and touch not the unclean thing; and I will receive you. And will be a Father unto you, and <u>you shall be my sons and daughters</u>, says the Lord Almighty.*

Then, Paul writes, you can cleanse or purify yourself from all the filthiness that is in the world, which can not only corrupt your flesh, but affect your spirit in the sense of hardening your heart. The key word in the passage *cleanse ourselves from all filthiness of the flesh...* is the word *from*—not *of*. God has sanctified us *of* all filthiness of the flesh, but we can keep ourselves pure *from* all the filthiness of the flesh.

I AM WHAT I AM

In the passage from 1 Corinthians 15, Paul teaches the same principle, but uses different language to make the point. After writing, *Be not deceived; evil communications corrupt good manners,* he writes, *Awake to righteousness, and sin not. For some have not the knowledge of God. I speak this to your shame.* [1 Corinthians 15:33-34]

Once again, the Bible directs us back to the truths of the new creature. Paul is saying, "Wake up to the fact that you are righteous by faith, and you will not sin." He then makes the comparison of their behavior to that of a lost person—to their shame.

From righteousness and holiness, to sanctification, time and time again, the Lord reminds us who we are and what we have in Him, so that we will not be destroyed by the storms when they come. As I have discussed throughout this book, the Bible teaches that the level of the victory in Christ we experience is related to a revelation of who we are in Christ—and until we begin to walk in these truths, we are ripe prey for the enemy who seeks to steal, kill, and destroy.

ABOVE ALL, TAKING THE SHIELD OF FAITH, WHEREWITH YOU SHALL BE ABLE TO QUENCH ALL THE FIERY DARTS OF THE WICKED.

Ephesians 6:16

14

It is Written...

WHERE-
WITHAL
SHALL A
YOUNG
MAN
CLEANSE
HIS WAY?
BY TAKING
HEED
THERETO
ACCORDING
TO YOUR
WORD.

Psalm 119:9

It is written, Man shall not live by bread alone, but by every word that proceeds out of the mouth of God.

MATTHEW 4: 4

The words of our Lord Jesus, when confronted and tempted to doubt His identity as the Son of God, should be as important to us as much as *For we walk by faith and not by sight.* [2 Corinthians 5:7] When the apostle Paul wrote this famous passage of Scripture, he was simply reiterating what the Lord had said in response to Satan's challenge. In other words we should say, "I live and walk by faith in God's word, and not what I see or detect by my physical senses."

The words of the Lord should be our mantra—our motto, as Paul wrote, *For I am the least of the apostles, that am not meet to be called an apostle, because I persecuted the church of God. But by the grace of God I am what I am...* [1 Corinthians 15:9-10] In other words, in the natural it wasn't right for him to be an apostle, but God had called him an apostle, and by His grace, he was an apostle.

Therefore, in the natural, you may not think it right or proper for you to be called holy, righteous, highly favored, more than a conqueror, beloved of God, blameless and unreproveable, a saint of God, partaker of the divine nature, son or daughter of God, heir of God and joint-heir with Christ, seated in the heavenly places with Christ, part of a chosen generation, His workmanship, ambassadors for Christ, complete in Him, and an overcomer of the world, but by the grace of God, you are what you are.

And because it is written, *Man shall not live by bread alone, but by every word that proceeds out of the mouth of God*, and that you *walk by faith and not by sight*, and that you have *set your affections on things above, not on things on the earth*, and that *you are dead, and your life is hid with Christ*, you can humbly receive and accept who God says you are, and then boldly say, "By the grace of God I am what I am."

Take these verses of Scripture and seal them in your heart, meditating on them day and night as it is written, *This book of the law shall not depart out of your mouth, but you shall meditate therein day and night, that you may observe to do according to all that is written therein. For then you shall make your way prosperous, and then you shall have good success.* [Joshua 1:8]

In Christ, we are:

- *part of a chosen generation, a royal priesthood, a holy nation, a peculiar people* [1 Peter 2:9]
- *partaker of the divine nature, having escaped the corruption that is in the world through lust* [2 Peter 1:4]

YOUR WORD HAVE I HID IN MY HEART THAT I MIGHT NOT SIN AGAINST YOU.

Psalm 119:11

- *sons of God* [John 1:12; 1 John 3:2]

- *more than conquerors* [Romans 8:37]

- *overcomers of the world* [1 John 5:4]

- *heirs of God, joint-heirs with Christ* [Romans 8:17]

- *the righteousness of God* [2 Corinthians 5:21]

- *not of this world* [John 17:14]

- *sanctified or set apart* [Acts 26:18; 1 Corinthians 1:2]

- *saints* [1 Corinthians 1:2; Acts 9:13]

- *ambassadors for Christ* [2 Corinthians 5:20]

- *the elect of God* [Colossians 3:12]

- *fellow-citizens with the saints, and of the household of God* [Ephesians 2:19]

- *temple of God* [1 Corinthians 3:16]

- *accepted in the beloved* [Ephesians 1:6]

- *highly favored* [Luke 1:28] (see note at the end of this section)

- *seated in heavenly places in Christ Jesus* [Ephesians 2:6]

- *to the praise of his glory* [Ephesians 1:12]

- *his workmanship created in Christ Jesus* [Ephesians 2:10]

- *sanctified and perfected forever* [Hebrews 10:14]

- *holy and without blame* [Ephesians 1:4]

- *complete in him* [Colossians 2:10]

- *as he is so are we in this world* [1 John 4:17]

- *holy and unblameable and unreproveable in his sight* [Colossians 1:22]

- *full of goodness, filled with all knowledge* [Romans 15:14]

I AM WHAT I AM

Note: When the angel Gabriel declared Mary *highly favored* (Luke 1:28) the Greek word used was *charitoo*, which is the same word used in Ephesians 1:6 to proclaim that we are *accepted in the beloved.*

In closing, my brothers and sisters, allow me to charge you once again to meditate on these passages of Scripture and *give yourself wholly to them that your profiting may appear to all.* [1 Timothy 4:15]

Walk confidently in God's word as Abraham did when God promised that he would be the father of many nations. Abraham placed a much higher value on what God had said than what he experienced or observed in the natural, and this is what we must do as it is written: *And being not weak in faith, he considered not his own body now dead, when he was about a hundred years old, neither the deadness of Sarah's womb. He staggered not at the promise of God through unbelief; but was strong in faith, giving glory to God; and being fully persuaded that, what he had promised, he was able also to perform. And therefore it was imputed to him for righteousness.* [Romans 4:19-22]

May the grace, peace, and mercy of our Lord Jesus Christ be with you all. Amen.

MY COVENANT WILL I NOT BREAK, NOR ALTER THE THING THAT IS GONE OUT OF MY LIPS.

Psalm 89:34

JEFF PATE is the founder of Branches of the Vine Ministries, a teaching and discipleship ministry located in North Carolina. Visit the ministry's web site at: www.bovministries.net.